Survivor

Hope

For my mother, Carmel Gibbons

Survivor

Michael Gibbons

LONDUBH BOOKS

All royalties from the sale of this book will go towards Ciara Brown's medical bills.

First published in 2014
by Londubh Books
18 Casimir Avenue, Harold's Cross, Dublin 6w, Ireland
www.londubh.ie

3 5 4 2 1

Origination by Londubh Books; cover by bluett
Printed by ScandBook AB, Falun Sweden

ISBN: 978-1-907535-44-4

This text is set out in Adobe Garamond Pro and Gotham.

Contents

Foreword

Ireland 2005 was in full Celtic Tiger mode. The country was drunk, delirious. My friends and I were fuelled by the belief that anything was possible. The Irish were taking over the world, well, certainly trying to buy or develop it. We didn't know it at the time but it was unsustainable and the crash was coming. We all know now what it's like to suffer the devastating effects of a crash. My crash just happened a few years sooner than everyone else's.

My two friends and I set out in a helicopter one morning. We were on top of the world, riding high. The crash came suddenly and was devastating. My two best friends were dead. The body bag was waiting for me but I was not ready to get into it and be zipped up.

This is a story of survival. In an instant you can have everything taken from you: health, mobility, livelihood. After the accident I fought back hard, especially against the monkey on my back that is PTSD. Your memory can be a devil. It may hide things from you but there is always something lurking in the shadows, ready to pounce like a mugger, attempting to steal from a vault of which you are the only one with the key. Your mind is your own, or so you think, but you soon realise you have a battle on your hands to hold on to it.

Survivor details the battles I fought and won but it is not a misery memoir: it is a book about life. Everyone is faced with challenges and obstacles. My family certainly has been. It is the way you react to and deal with those challenges that defines you and how you will live your life.

The helicopter crash was a transformative experience and in

the end it enriched my life. I would love if my dead friends were still alive to see me live out my dreams but I am not submerged in a swamp of regret and recrimination because they are no longer beside me. I have accepted that they are gone. After a traumatic event, acceptance is the only way to get on to the path that will take you forward.

When a crash comes you realise what is important. I am sure a lot of people in post-Celtic Tiger Ireland have come to the same realisation as me. The most important thing of all is family.

The remarkable selflessness, kindness and love shown to me by my mother Carmel Gibbons and my two sisters, Karen Brown and Norrie Malone, are some of the main reasons I came through to the other side. They nursed me back to health. My mother was as strong as iron throughout it all, always on hand to distribute the wisdom her own life circumstances have imprinted on her. My sister Karen was always there for me and I know she always will be. My sister Norrie thought nothing of uprooting herself from her home more than an hour away and moving in to take care of me after the accident, although she had a new baby at the time. I could not have made the recovery I did without their love and constant support.

My nephew and nieces are all remarkable kids. Oisín never ceases to amaze me by the way he can turn his hand to anything: dancing, sports, engineering. The dancing definitely did not come from the Gibbons side of the family. Rachel will some day ride for Ireland. Her passion for horses is infectious but watching her jump may give me a coronary. As for Laura, I think we may have the next Beyoncé in the family. Her enthusiasm for drama and theatre does not appear to have come from the Gibbons side either – but, then again, maybe part of it did.

This book is the final element of a bucket list I made after finding out that my two best friends had been killed in the helicopter crash. I was lying in intensive care and my future looked bleak. What happened since has been an incredible journey that I have a really strong desire to share.

It took three remarkable people to get my story of survival to publication. One is Christy O'Connor, one of my closest friends since college days, himself a bestselling author. He greeted my first manuscript with 'Boss, this is not good enough.' It wasn't and Christy's contribution in taking the book to another level was invaluable.

Jo O'Donoghue of Londubh Books is another: a total lady and great company. She was welcomed unconditionally by everyone in the Gibbons household whilst pursuing and navigating our family's past history and present story, editing the book to its full potential.

My best friend, Ronan Daly, was a catalyst for every decision I made and I know I would not have been able to make such good decisions without him.

Thanks to my friends Jimmy Harlowe (the comedian) and Jo O'Rourke, who through all this never lost their ability to make me laugh and feel good; to Stella and Chuck in NYC; to all the gang in Columbia University – Ling, Margarita, Jamie 'Like Like', Tehmina, Cami and many more – all of whom played their part in showing me how one can really live in the city that never sleeps.

To Fozzy (Shane), Scotty (Salvadoran), Jared, Katie, Adam and Bonnie in Miami – my favourite Latinos in the world. Thanks for some great times.

Finally, there is one special person to whom I wish to express my deepest gratitude and appreciation. Once you have gone through tough experiences you can never forget them. You have to accept them, understand them and never be afraid of them. Then you can understand what life is all about. It's about picking yourself up time and time again. This is what my mother did. I did it too. And now my niece Ciara, who was born with no lower limbs, has done it. Ciara has been an inspiration to us all and she inspires me every day of my life. She makes me determined to make the most out of every minute of every day, to appreciate every second I have on this earth.

Life is for living. And I want to live it to the absolute maximum.

Prologue

Late November 2013 in Stirling, the heart of Scotland's central belt and a jewel in its historical and cultural crown. It's damp and cold but the tingle of Christmas is running through the spine of the city and the heritage mile that links Stirling's old town with its vibrant city centre is buzzing. So am I.

This was once Scotland's capital, where wars were fought and monarchs ruled in splendour for three centuries. As my girlfriend Natalie and I stroll the heritage mile, we pass beautifully preserved mediaeval and Renaissance churches and mansions, along cobbled streets with period street furniture and Victorian ironwork. Then we amble along the 'Back Walk', a scenic pathway around the castle and old town.

As soon as you enter Stirling's iconic castle, with its spectacular cliff-top location, you get a strong sense of history and nation-hood. It is almost as if we are living the dream because we more or less have the place to ourselves. Several Scottish monarchs were crowned in Stirling. We feel like one of them.

I want the weekend to be special so we have booked into Culcreuch Castle, outside the village of Fintry, near Loch Lomond. That afternoon we sit in our room, aptly named the Baron's Suite, and look out at acres of woodland, set against the backdrop of the Trossachs and the Highlands, where the legends of William Wallace and Rob Roy had their origin.

Later in the evening, we make the short journey to Edinburgh. After a romantic meal, we go for drinks to a bar not far from the restaurant. As soon as I walk in the door, I know something is not right. The place is busy but there is an eerie silence. Everyone seems to be facing the opposite side of the bar. I shrug and order two glasses of wine. A few seconds later, I notice that Natalie's gaze is fixed intently on something behind me. I turn around, suddenly realising that everyone is transfixed by the live images on the TV screens. I soon understand why the mood is so sombre: the scene of the disaster relayed on the screens is not much more than an hour's drive away, in Glasgow.

I look closer and the pieces of the jigsaw began to fit. A helicopter has come down, crashing into a pub, the Clutha Vaults, on the north bank of the River Clyde. The three people who were aboard the helicopter are already confirmed dead but the death toll is surely set to rise. A ska band, Esperanza, was playing in the pub at the time of the crash and, according to reports, a hundred and twenty people were in the building. The mass of rubble I can see on the TV screen tells me that some of them won't make it out.

In an instant, the hairs stand on the back of my neck. The memories come flooding back: the yellow police tape, the phalanx of fire-fighters and rescue personnel, the sense of desolation, the hopelessness. The frantic fear of death.

It feels as if a nightmare has suddenly revisited me, to trigger a raft of emotions and fears that will cripple me. But I gather myself and quickly snap out of it. My first thoughts are with the victims and their families. The survivors who are now battling through hell – I know exactly how they feel. I know the terror and torture that have come to visit them.

My initial reaction is like a jolt from an electric current. I feel that sense of helplessness and dread again. Dozens of imaginings jostle in my head, stirred by the event the TV cameras have allowed me to witness. But I have learned to steel my mind and insulate myself from the shock of seeing the destruction a helicopter crash can wreak.

Across the table, I can see the anxiety on Natalie's face. She is distressed by what has happened but also anxious about the impact this may have on me. We are in Scotland for a romantic weekend, to enjoy each other's company, to leave the worries and stresses of life behind us for forty-eight hours. But the anxieties of life appear to have followed us like a stealth bomber. I reassure her that I am fine and my thoughts remain with the people trapped underneath the mesh of steel and the concrete rubble.

When I speak I am relaxed and considered. I say to Natalie, 'In the end, life is a series of memories. And I want my memories to be as good as possible.'

As I watch the news, it would have been easy for me to become shocked and stunned by the images, to smell the fumes and feel the fear in my mind's eye, to hear my own screams, see myself lying on my back, slipping in and out of consciousness. Any time I was conscious the fear of dying was threatening to engulf me.

All around me was carnage. Desperation. Desolation. Of my two best friends who were with me, Mark was already dead, Damien was calling the emergency services in an attempt to save us.

If you ask anyone who has ever piloted a helicopter, or even travelled in one, the result is more than likely a body count when one goes down Back in July 2005, the body count was two. The body bag was being prepared for me as well but I wasn't ready to get into it and be zipped up.

The collateral cost of survival against the odds is post traumatic stress disorder (PTSD), with symptoms like guilt, panic attacks, nightmares, waking up in a cold sweat. But I don't have any of that. Of course I often feel loneliness and sadness but that is the extent of it for me. Every person has a survival personality. Mine is strong. I'd like to think it's as strong as oak. I never knew it was until I met disaster. We all rely on our survival personality at times of crisis and if you are not willing to engage or activate that mode, PTSD will come into your life and steal everything you have.

Do I miss Mark and Damien? More than I can put into words.

But when I see the footage of that helicopter crash and all the emotions and memories of Mark and Damien came flooding back, I have a sense of perspective in my life, not panic. My survival personality takes over. My subconscious is processing all these emotions, sifting through my own experiences, filtering what is important and what is not. I am living life in the here and now, not chained to what happened in the past.

Instead I recollect all the great times I had with my two best friends. All the funny stories. They are no longer here but I have long since accepted that. Of course there is heartbreak but I don't dwell on the sadness of their not being here, the fact that we no longer share our lives. I celebrate what we had and take strength from that. Acceptance is one of the most essential things in life. There is no reverse, no turning back the clock, no second chance.

For me, clarity came after crashing out of the sky at approximately a hundred and fifteen miles an hour. It involved overcoming catastrophic injuries, dealing with the pain of losing my best friends who were also my brother and father figures, facing down a myriad legal difficulties, the curse of boredom.

Now I think I have survivor delight. I wake up every morning energised by the challenge of the day ahead. I went back to college, got my master's degree from Columbia University, made a little money in a handful of business ventures.

My mother taught my two sisters and me to draw a line under experiences, not to drown in our emotions, searching for answers that will lead only to frustration, to move on but never forget what we had gone through. This is life. We have to accept tragic circumstances when they occur.

Human beings have an inbuilt capacity for survival. Our brains work at lightning speed when we engage our survival personality. As we go through life, the human mind is the most powerful weapon at our disposal. It's amazing how fast our brains can process lived experiences. If we have lived them – and learned from them – our brain will use these memories the next time we face similar challenges.

When I was younger, before the crash, I had everything anyone could want: the girl, money, my own house, a licence to travel to the four corners of the world. But youth is often wasted on the young. We think we know everything when in fact we know little. In the days after the accident, I remember thinking I was all alone. I told my mother as much as I lay in the hospital bed with a fractured spinal L3, fractured forehead, elbow, toe, sternum, rib, a collapsed lung and a body that looked almost completely black and blue. I thought I was finished. I was looking into the abyss of a bleak future. My business was gone. My life had been turned upside down. I had broken nearly every bone in my body. But I got up and walked ten days after crashing into the side of a mountain. I got up because I needed to get up. We all need to get up when we fall. The world has no place for people who lie down.

Three other lives have been claimed in Glasgow and, given the circumstances of that helicopter crash, the death toll is bound to rise in the coming hours and days. That gruesome reality is inevitable. My heart bleeds for those people but as I sip my wine and chat to Natalie, I am as tuned into those TV screens as anyone else inside the pub. I don't want to run or hide from what is happening. I want to learn more about the tragedy, about what might have caused the accident, about the people inside the helicopter who have been killed.

As the hours pass, the information slowly percolates through. It was a police helicopter that had been involved in the search for a suspected trespasser on railway lines around Eglinton Toll, about a mile south of the crash site. The Scottish Fire and Rescue Service has more than a hundred fire fighters at the scene as they attempt to rescue people trapped in the building. Those initially rescued are taken to a nearby Holiday Inn and the casualties to various local hospitals. Some of the injuries are classed as extremely serious. I watch the gruesome scenes with compassion and pain in my heart but also with clarity. At least three people have died in a helicopter crash. Once I was in a situation where I might have died like them. But I got that second chance. And I don't intend to waste it.

1

Life Repeats Itself

Not too long ago Father Martin Glynn from Westside parish came rushing over to my mother in such haste that she assumed he was enquiring about my wellbeing after the helicopter accident. Father Glynn told Mam that he was reading a book about a guy who met his father for the first time. He said he often recalled the day I was in a similar situation. That day was burned into Father Glynn's mind because it had totally altered his expectations around events like this.

When I was that guy in the book, after I'd met my father for the first time, Father Glynn greeted me as if I'd been told the third secret of Fatima. He animatedly asked me about the meeting, expecting to hear details of a life-changing experience, as if some genetic catalyst had suddenly created an unbreakable bond between father and son.

In a feel-good novel, that is how the encounter would be, a script a Hollywood writer would adapt for a soft ending. But for me, the reality was completely different. The best way to describe the moment was like meeting a perfectly pleasant man on a bus. You talk for a while, shoot the breeze, nothing heavy. Then you arrive at your stop and get off. You forget about the man you met and go back to your life.

When I told Father Glynn that the meeting meant nothing to me, he was puzzled. The look on his face suggested that I had poured ink over the script he had written in his mind. The

Hollywood movie didn't have the perfect ending after all.

There is a simple way of looking at this: to deal with loss, you first have to embrace acceptance. Of course I would have loved to know the man. But that time was lost. It was long gone and I needed to accept that fact. I really mean it when I say that I wished my father the best but there was no place in my life for yesterday. The past is the past. It's what's in front of you that matters.

I learned that from a very early age. I knew that my life, and that of my family, was not going to be easy. My mother and father separated when I was three months old. I never really bothered about the details of why it happened. We moved on as a family. Anyone who has met Carmel Gibbons will understand why she instilled that philosophy in me and my two sisters. It might sound ultra-simple but we always adopted that mantra as a family and it was one of the best coping skills I had at my disposal when I was recovering from the helicopter crash.

I love my mother unconditionally. She is a remarkable woman, always a survivor. After she and my father split up, we went to live with my grandmother. The state did not want to know about us or our plight so in an attempt to highlight our desperate need for a house of our own we moved into a caravan on the banks of the river Corrib in Galway. We were like gypsies. My mother had no income and we had lost everything but at least we had a roof over our heads and we were together. But most important of all, my mother had the one thing in life that fuelled her drive and the absolute fire in her heart – her three children and the love she felt for them.

She once told me a story about her life during that period (she was only twenty-five). She was penniless, alone and scared. The living space in the caravan was barely enough for one, never mind an adult and three young children. One evening, my mother put my two sisters to bed and eventually got me to sleep. I had been crying all evening and it was late and cold when she pulled the fold-out bed down from the wall of the caravan to rest her weary head and tired body. The bed jackknifed into the wall, knocking her to the floor. As she lay there, stunned by the impact, she put her hands over her face and burst into floods of tears. Her world was caving in. It felt as if it had collapsed, like the bed.

Then she looked at her children and stopped crying. My mother had love on her side. That was all she needed. She had everything to live for and knew then that she would be able to overcome any obstacle in her way. It was this kind of attitude and will to survive and prosper that she passed on to me: learn to accept things if you can't change them. There were plenty of tough times but the only story that counts for me is that my mother raised three children on her own, no easy task in Ireland in the 1970s and 1980s.

Carmel Gibbons

'I had Karen before I was eighteen. Mike was only three months old when we split up and we had to live in a caravan and in the Rahoon flats (third floor, forty-two steps, no lift, three kids, one rabbit), probably the worst area in Galway at the time. I made myself a solemn promise, "I'm going to make a job out of this." I wanted to make sure that they were never in trouble with the law or anything like that. I dedicated my life to them. I never did anything apart from rearing them. Now looking back, I wonder how we did it. How did we manage for money? I got some payment from the state. I took cleaning jobs here and there. I didn't know any other way of life. You worked hard to make ends meet. You paid your bill as it came in the door. We got the house I still live in now and I wouldn't leave there. It was the kids' home and eventually I got to buy out the house.

'The children worked from when they were very young. They had to. There wasn't time for them to get involved with other kids from around the area who got into trouble. That is where

Mikey's stubbornness comes from, his drive and willpower. When he started going out as a teenager, he had to be home at a certain time. He might have to be home at 2am. He might be home at 1.30 but would wait outside the gate until two. Karen sometimes came in and asked him what he was doing and he would say, "I'm waiting for the stroke of two.'"

Believe me, life repeats itself. You will face the same situations again and again. And as long as you are constantly learning from these experiences, you are programming your disaster personality for when a crisis happens.

When I told my mother that I wanted to meet my father, she was fully supportive. Our first port of call was the local priest. If you want to find someone in Ireland, forget about the Gardaí. The priests know everyone. The CIA or FBI wouldn't be in their league.

It didn't take the priests long to track down my father. A meeting was arranged in Gort, a town in south Galway, half-way between the places where we lived. Two priests – one from each side – also attended the meeting, covering all bases, like the US marines. As they saw it they were doing their Christian duty. The priests and the Catholic Church in Ireland have been hammered in the past number of years after decades of sexual and physical abuse were uncovered. Yet in the past priests were often the only people you could turn to in bad times and they were there for me and my family when we needed them.

A couple of weeks before the meeting, I found out that I had a stepbrother. I knew absolutely nothing about him. How would I? As a family, we never lived in the past and I never asked whether I might have stepbrothers or stepsisters. That line of thinking was so irrelevant to us that we simply never entertained the possibility.

When the time came, I was excited about meeting my stepbrother. And guess what his name was? Yeah, you're right,

Michael Gibbons. So we have a Michael Gibbons Senior, Junior and Younger in our family.

We met in a bar in Gort. My father was friendly and cordial. Charming. Then he introduced me to my stepbrother, Michael.

Meeting my younger stepbrother was confusing. Beforehand, I had put little or no thought into how I might feel about that moment. I didn't think about all the possibilities; how he might look; if he bore any resemblance to me; if he had some of the same traits; that there might be a spark that would immediately connect us. What really stuck with me was his name. It seemed strange to me that my father would call his two sons the same name.

After he and my mother split up, my father took me and my sisters to live with him and we were separated from my mother. I don't remember anything about that time. My father employed a nanny to take care of us but my sisters often told me how difficult I made her life. I refused to eat anything she gave me. When the nanny tried to force-feed me, I used to spit the food straight back out at her.

My mother was young. Like most people in Ireland at that time, she had little education. Yet she had the resolve and determination to take a high-court case, with the result that we, her children, came back to live with her.

Studies show that children develop much of their personality during their earliest years. That period when I was away from my mother had a profound effect on my personality. For a start, it created an unbreakable bond between my mother and me. It also instilled in me an iron determination to succeed.

That force of will developed further from watching my mother struggle to raise three children with very little money. We were pre-programmed for coping with failure and disaster and moving on. My mother had moved on from difficult experiences and made a success of her life. When she stood at the foot of my bed the morning after the crash, she didn't just offer great love and support: she gave me the inspiration to recover fully.

It is something she has been doing all her life.

After I met my stepbrother, I asked the priests to take the boy away so that I could talk to my father. We talked for about thirty minutes. I can't say it was an enjoyable experience. It was sort of weird. I had become so detached from most of what he was saying that I honestly don't know what I felt afterwards. I decided to be friendly and listen to what he had to say. I had come to the meeting with an open mind and kept that sense of clarity, before, during and after the meeting. I saw no reason to veer off the path I was following. We had a happy life at home. I was doing well and trying to get into college. I accepted the facts as they were; on one hand, I had a happy family life; on the other, I knew engaging with my father had the potential to affect my life. The decision was easy. Acceptance was easy. I moved on, away from the risk.

Although I was only seventeen at the time, I was the head of the house. My two sisters had done well and had good careers in the bank. My mother had her house. I had a part-time job and had finally grasped the importance of going to college if I really wanted to move forward in life.

I had made it through the most difficult part of my teenage years without a brother or father figure. I was becoming my own man. My natural instinct was to turn my back on the chance of developing a relationship with my father and stepbrother. Father Glynn was shocked by how I reacted. To me there was nothing shocking about it. It came down to one word – clarity.

I admit I had the same feelings of curiosity and intrigue that adopted children often have – or so people told me before I met my father. This stems from the search for an identity during adolescence, when you are trying to put all the pieces of the jigsaw together. As you get older, you realise that you cannot put all the pieces together. I soon realised I had nothing to be curious about. You may wish for something to happen but you soon accept that the wish is not going to come true. I had a choice whether or not to open up to my father and stepbrother and tell them about my life but I chose not to. After my initial curiosity was satisfied, I had no interest in knowing about their lives either.

My sisters travelled a different route. They tracked my father down to a pub where he drank. My eldest sister has a striking resemblance to my mother and my father was taken aback when he saw her. When she approached him there was an argument. To get closure on the matter, I was cold and calculated in what I decided to do. I enlisted the help of Mike, my best friend at the time, who had access to a car. I knew where some relatives on my father's side lived so we took a chance and called on them. I arrived outside the house, out of the blue, and rang the doorbell. An aunt whom I had never seen before answered the door. I casually introduced myself. Although taken aback at first, she introduced me to her family and they were all very friendly and helpful in steering me in the right direction.

When we got to the house, I asked Mike to stay in the car. A cousin answered the door and I introduced myself. I asked to see my father and told him calmly that it was nice to have met him, but that we were very happy as a family and did not want anything more to do with him. I wished him and Michael Junior the very best for the future.

I like to think that I have a powerful aura and I am sure he was left in no doubt about the sincerity of my statement that I did not want to have anything more to do with him. He could probably detect it in my voice, read it in my expression. He went back to living his own life and we never met him again.

I realised that my father was a stranger in my life, nothing more. He was my flesh and blood, nothing more. I know some people can develop amazing relationships with a biological parent after many years. Many of them speak of the profound chemistry when they first meet. I don't know if I ever wanted that. I suppose some people never feel complete without knowing their biological parents. I never felt this way. It never came up. All I ever wanted or needed was provided by my remarkable mother.

Other people, like me, feel nothing when they are reunited with their biological parents. When I look back on that time now, the calmness I felt that day when I cut my father entirely out of my life was my survival mentality taking control of the situation.

I learned from this experience that you have to be able to deal with loss in a realistic way. You embrace the lessons learned and move on. You can't live in the past, I didn't realise it at the time but this was a key learning tool that I would use again later on in life.

When you are faced with trauma, your subconscious looks for a grip as you try to stop yourself from falling to pieces. It hunts for past experience, or pieces of experience, to fuse together a logic that can make sense of what has happened. This is where we get what we call 'gut feelings'. My experience with my father gave me the skills to say goodbye to another father figure, Mark, as well as a brother figure, Damien.

2

Do It

Do you remember the movie *Pulp Fiction*? Sure you do. Everyone does. Do you remember the Vincent Vega character played by John Travolta? The big guy who walked with a kind of shuffle, swinging his shoulders slightly backwards and forwards. Damien had perfected a similar walk. In my mind's eye, I can see him doing that walk and the memory always brings a smile to my face.

I can still vividly remember the first time I met Damien Bergin. Jimmy, my oldest friend, went off to college in Tralee, then to Cardiff to finish his studies before returning to Galway. When I met up with him, he was with this big beast of a man, Damien. By beast, I mean Vincent Vegaesque. He was huge and he had an aura to match. It was no surprise that his favourite move was *Pulp Fiction*.

I remember one Saturday having lunch with Mark and another friend, John. As usual Damien was late. We joked that he would be late for his own funeral. At that moment he walked into the Front Door pub and everyone's gaze was magnetically drawn towards him, as if a vision was standing before them.

He was wearing a pressed pink shirt, with a pink jumper casually thrown across his shoulders. Damien was so big he could just about fit through the door. He appeared to be blocking out the sun behind him. He strode towards us with his Vincent Vega shuffle, a smile that lit up the entire room, and an aura that shimmered and put the rest of us mere mortals in the shade. Then he laughed and we laughed with him.

That was Damien. Nothing was ever a problem. In fact, the words 'No problem' were his answer to everything. If he didn't use that expression, he'd use the famous line Nike patented. Except he would drop the 'Just ' and say, 'do it'. Invariably I did it but it was much more fun if Damien and Mark were with me. Mark was married with kids so it was often left to Damien and me to 'do it'. The only thing was that we invariably overdid it.

One Christmas, Damien and I decided to go to Australia for a month, even though neither of us had much money at the time. All his money was tied up in a pending property venture and mine had been invested in a company. However, our mindsets dictated the terms of engagement: life is there to be lived, so 'do it'. What else would we do?

En route, we were delayed during a stopover in Paris and were put up in a hotel for the night. Our plan of action was very basic: go to the bar, drink at least two bottles of wine and party with the other people from the flight.

We got hammered drunk. The next thing I remember is waking up in the lobby. In my underpants. I have always been prone to sleepwalking, especially when I have something on my mind. I needed a strategy so I explained to the receptionist that I had been locked out of my room. When she asked me for the room number, I couldn't remember it. After racking my brain, I gave her a number which I thought might be the correct one. As she didn't have a list of the names of the occupants in front of her, she handed me the key.

When I opened the bedroom door, I could see that the bed was empty, which suggested to me that my brain was not as fried as I thought it was. But as I was about to collapse on to the mattress, an Asian guy jumped up from the other side of the bed. He was about sixty but his actions belied his age. After roaring and shouting in a foreign language, he assumed a martial arts stance, all of a sudden looking like Mr Myagie in *The Karate Kid*.

I took up a boxing position and there was an immediate stand-off. He was speaking Chinese while I told him in my Irish brogue to relax, as I casually retreated to the door. I opened it and ran for my life. I headed straight for the stairs. My brain had already computed that the elevator was not an option because I would have to wait for it and risk getting decapitated by a karate kick from Mr Myagie.

I flew down the stairs and arrived at the reception in a lather of sweat. I was completely out of breath but my survival personality had kicked in – we use it more than we think in everyday life. The receptionist looked at me as if I had two heads and enquired about my wellbeing. All I was concerned about was Mr Myagie flying around the corner with his wax-on, wax-off moves and taking me to the cleaners. In order to sort out the mess and save me from a potential hiding, the receptionist had to wake the airline representative.

Next morning when I arrived in the dining hall a furious airline rep raced over to me, asking if I was Mr Gibbons. I knew how serious she was because I could see spittle almost splattering from her lips. I immediately denied that I was Mr Gibbons. I asked her why she wanted to speak to him. Apparently he had been wandering around the hotel in the middle of the night, semi-naked, going into strangers' rooms and waking them up. 'That's ridiculous behaviour,' I replied. 'You really need to take that up with him.'

'I most certainly will,' she said. 'Do you know who he is?'

'Do you remember that very large man from Ireland?'

Of course she did, who didn't?

'Well, that's Mr Gibbons.'

'Right, I'll speak to him as soon as I see him.'

I wanted the best seat in the house for this show but I had to be strategic about the seat I took. I was hungover and starving so I wanted breakfast but I needed to be out of sight and near an exit so I could get the hell out of the place if they came looking for me.

'Mr Gibbons' strolled into the dining room like he owned the place, forty-five minutes late for breakfast. The airline rep made straight for him and started shouting. Mr Gibbons, confused, shuffled away from her like Vincent Vega, trying to ignore her.

But this woman was tenacious. She grabbed Mr Gibbons by the arm and started pointing at him in a very judgemental manner. Think Miss Piggy meets Hulk Hogan.

By now, tears were cascading down my face as I watched the show. Mr Gibbons had no clue as to what was going on and kept shaking his head. Eventually he'd had enough. He looked down at her, pointed his finger and shouted, 'I am not Mr fucking Gibbons, you crazy woman.'

Total silence enveloped the dining room.

'You're crazy,' he said. 'Now get the fuck away from me.'

He walked towards the breakfast bar. The rep knew better than to follow him. When he spotted me behind all the camouflage, he started to laugh. Within seconds, both of us were bent over, tears running down our faces. Damien had a way of bending over when hilarity kicked in. Next minute he was telling me he was going to get sick but his condition suddenly improved when I told him the background to the story.

He often teased me about the incident, calling me the naked wanderer, and the story certainly shortened the long flight to Australia. By the time we arrived in Cairns, we had made plans to book a camper van to tour the Gold Coast. At that stage, we were living on borrowed money. We didn't care. We were going to catch the Celtic Tiger by the tail and shake him for all he was worth once we got home. Our liquidity problem would only be short-lived but it was still time to budget and live in the real world. We weren't interested. We went out that night and blew a small fortune, chasing girls who were far too young for us. We felt invincible. No wonder with the egos we had.

We woke up the next day with hangovers that would have killed an elephant. The pounding inside my skull eventually got a clear message through to my brain. It was time to be practical as we proceeded with our adventure. I insisted that we get a two-man camper van. Damien was having none of it – he wanted a luxury van that would sleep six.

I stood my ground and eventually won the argument. He knew all about cars so he went off to hire the camper van while I stayed in the pub. Bad call.

Half an hour later, Damien pulled up in a huge van, like something out of MTV *Cribs* – on wheels. He was wearing dark sunglasses, the music was booming through the window and he looked like the cat that had got the cream. Luxury was an understatement. This thing was big enough for P Diddy and his entire entourage.

All I could do was laugh. But I was afraid we might kill each other if we were stuck in this vehicle for three weeks with no other company. I felt that there was only one option; we needed women to fill it. Damien laughed and agreed. He nodded towards the van and immediately christened it 'the camper of love'.

To recruit some 'love', we made our way to an internet café and drew up an A4 poster. It read something like this.

> Two Irish Guys Looking for Girls to Share Petrol Costs Only in Six-Berth Camper to Brisbane
>
> No Drama Allowed
>
> Must Be Able to Handle Hangovers
>
> Fuel Money Only Required

We lost the run of ourselves and thought we were two Andy Warhols and decorated the poster with pictures of camper vans, drink, hungover people, happy faces. As soon as we finished creating our masterpiece, we photocopied it and pinned up a copy in every hostel in central Cairns. Our work got prime position on those notice boards as Damien ripped up other notices to make way for our masterpiece.

We got a few replies and scheduled interviews for the following evening. We had set criteria in mind for the kind of companions we wanted. The initial batch did not meet our standards. Two of the interviewees were teachers from Ireland. They were nice girls but Damien put his foot down. He said that they would be counting our drinks and have us living off a timetable. I'm not saying he wanted strippers or alcoholics but he had his own logic and it was often best not to argue with him. The following morning, I was asleep when I heard a knock on the door of the van. I had to drag myself out of bed but opening the door was like splashing cold water over my face. Standing in front of me were three beautiful girls, clad in short skirts and bikinis tops. As far as I was concerned, this was the profile we were looking for. I immediately sold them the idea and arranged to meet them at the pool at 2pm.

I said nothing to Damien. Not knowing that we had already hit the jackpot, he had been bitching and moaning about our lack of HR skills, our inability to attract the bees despite our huge pot of honey. The types of girl we wanted may be plentiful in Miami but they were in short supply in Cairns.

We were both at the pool when the three beauties arrived. They dropped a crate of beer beside us, then hugged and kissed me. Damien was taking all this in, not knowing what was going down. A few minutes later, when they realised that he was also going to be part of the camper of love, they began to smother him with hugs and smear lipstick all over his cheeks. When the penny dropped, he nodded over to me. We definitely had our girls. We had the time of our lives with them. We did it.

Mark Reilly may have been seen as a real high-flyer around Galway but he had a multi-layered character. He was religious and was even part of a bible study group not long before he died. He was a brilliant soccer player and had trials with Arsenal when he was only fifteen. When he didn't make it as a soccer player, he became a stone mason.

Mark grew up in Drogheda but work brought him to Galway in the late 1980s. His friends say that he was brilliant at his job. I haven't a clue about stonework but if you stand in the Front Door bar and take a look around at some of the decorative stonework you can appreciate his talent. Or in another pub someone might say to you, 'Mark Reilly put down that floor you're standing on.' They were proud to be associated with him in any way.

Mark's trade, along with his infectious personality, led him into business. He first met his great friend and future business partner John Mannion in 1990 when John had taken over his first pub in Galway, Monroe's Tavern. Mark was the contractor for the reconstruction work and he and John instantly hit it off. When John took over the famous Róisín Dubh in Dominic Street in 1993, Mark became his partner in the venture.

In 1996, Mark and John bought Mrs Murphy's shop on Cross Street, which is now the site of the renowned Front Door bar. They bought the bar licence but didn't have the funds to develop it at the time so they leased it to Hugh O'Regan for a few years. He built the pub up into a huge business before Mark and John took it over in 2001. (Hugh O'Regan passed away in 2013. He and Mark were great friends and, like Mark, he would never see anyone stuck.) In the meantime (in 1997) they had bought Sonny Molloy's shop, which was known as Naughton's, in a prime location in Galway city.

Although Mark and John sold their leasehold on the Róisín

Dubh in 2004, when Mark died he was half-owner of the Front Door and half-owner of Tom Sheridan's pub in Knocknacarra. He was fairly well off but that never changed his personality. Everyone took to Mark. No one had a bad word to say about him. He was like Damien in that everyone wanted to be around him. When Mark and Damien were together, they were like a magnet – people gravitated to them.

Mark had a natural way with people and huge charm. He was a great storyteller and would have everyone in stitches laughing at his stories. But his greatest trait was his generosity. He had huge heart and had even guaranteed a business loan for me. He was a good judge of people and would never see anyone stuck.

It was people who made him tick and he was able to forge relationships with people from all walks of life. His goodness and kindness were so great that people were always trying to reciprocate in some way.

As with most friendships, there were factors big and small that bound us together. When I got to know Mark well he was going through a bad time. He had broken up with his wife, while I had come out of a long-term relationship. We seemed to be on the same wavelength at that period in our lives.

Another bond between us was the fact that his second child, Jodie, suffered from asthma. I worked in the medical sales sector so I knew plenty of specialists in that area. A company I was working for had a specialist who did work for them and I put Mark and Jodie in contact with him. This specialist had the time to explain exactly what was wrong. I was only too happy to oblige but Mark could not get over the fact that someone he barely knew would go to that kind of trouble for him. To me it was no big deal but to him it was massive.

We became friends and he literally would have done anything for me. When I decided to go out on my own in business, he guaranteed me around £125,000 he had invested in an apartment in London. He essentially gambled that apartment on my venture but he explained it by saying, 'When I was stuck, you did what you could for me, now I am repaying you.' That was how he looked at it, plain and simple.

I never had any interest in sport but Mark continued to play soccer into his late forties. He regularly played five-a-side games in Drom, Salthill-Devon's base, and he always retained a huge affection for Arsenal. When he spoke about soccer, everyone listened to what he had to say.

Ultimately, though, he was a great family man and doted on his three kids, Gemma, Jodie and Mark junior. I still find it difficult to accept that Mark left three young children behind. It doesn't seem fair. The pain that family experienced often creeps into my mind. It is an embodiment of how cruel life can be.

Eight weeks before his death, Mark and his wife reached agreement on a settlement. He was beginning a new chapter in his life but in reality all he cared about was the kids. When he had them to stay, he would spend two days preparing and trying to be the perfect father.

When Mark left home, he moved in with Damien in Forster Street in Galway. He was a few years older than Damien and he probably saw himself as a father figure for him. In truth Mark was a father figure for many people he came into contact with. I'm sure others saw that aspect of the relationship too. This was the type of guy Mark was. He looked out for everyone and made a huge impression on people.

Every year, John Mannion organises a gathering on the anniversary of Mark's death, which was also his birthday. What seems amazing to John is that as time goes by the list of people attending get longer rather than shorter. People still come out of the woodwork with stories about how Mark helped them in one way or another and want to join the gathering. I haven't been at that event for a few years now because I have been in the US but

I always hear the stories. The gathering takes place in the bar that Mark half-owned, Sheridan's in Knocknacarra. Mark was heavily involved in the building of that pub. He lived down the road so it was his home from home.

Mark, Damien and I cemented our friendships during a golden time in Ireland. If you had ambition and drive the streets were paved with gold during the Celtic Tiger years. You did not even need money. Debt was good and the banks were even better at encouraging you to take on more. You could be as dangerous without money as you could be with it.

The good times were going to go on for ever. Everyone was high on optimism. Everyone was buying property. Little did we know how it would end. During the boom, we kept riding the tide, surfing the crest of any wave that appeared. We were always looking for the next deal, the next big buck.

As a successful publican and property developer, Mark was by far the wealthiest of the three of us. Damien had received planning for a big development and was well on his way to becoming a millionaire. I was part-owner of a medium-sized company.

We enjoyed life. We loved one another's company. Spending time with the two lads was like a cross between *The Sopranos* and *60 minutes*: fun, food, drink, laughter, teasing – and, of course, talk about women. We always loved to meet up for lunch or dinner but the fun and enjoyment we had was nourishment for the soul. We were real friends. The strength of that friendship was borne out by the loyalty the two lads showed towards me. Not only was Mark backing my business venture, Damien was going to bankroll me for a pending legal case. I never had a father or brother but the bond I had with Mark and Damien was like having a father and brother as my two best friends. It was a unique connection. We loved life. We lived the dream. I never thought the dream would end so suddenly.

3

Crash

The first Tall Ships event was held in 1956, when a race of twenty of the world's remaining large sailing ships was organised as a farewell to the era of great sailing. That race was from Torquay in Devon to Lisbon but public interest was so strong that the organisers founded the Sail Training International Association to direct the planning of future events. Since then Tall Ships races have occurred annually in various parts of the world, with millions of spectators.

When the 49th annual race began in Waterford in July 2005, it was the kind of global event that gave Irish people a perfect opportunity to celebrate. Publicity around the event was huge and Damien's antennae were tuned into that frequency. One night the week before the festival we were out together and Damien suggested that the three of us should go. We could rent a friend's helicopter, stay the night and have the best seats in the house for the start of the race the following day. Mark and I looked at each other. There was no need for a discussion. We were already making plans.

When we left Galway for Waterford the following Friday, Mark was late so I took the front seat beside Damien. I wanted to sit up front anyway but there was an unwritten rule in our helicopter flights that whoever sat beside the pilot for the first part of a journey took the back seat for the return trip.

After the euphoria of lift-off, a helicopter flight can get very boring. Being inside a helicopter is not conducive to conversation because it is far too noisy. Being up front at least strips some of the boredom away because you have a panoramic view. As soon as we got nearer the coastline that vista stretched ahead of us, a beautiful blue canvas.

Because we had left it so late to decide to go to the festival, we had booked no accommodation. There was nothing available in Waterford so we ended up staying in New Ross. We got a taxi into Waterford that evening. It was idyllic. The weather was warm, the atmosphere buzzing. With the ships providing the perfect backdrop, the setting was pure magic. We didn't even drink that much. We didn't need to. We were drunk on the moment. Mark and I had three drinks in a local bar before we headed back to our hotel at around 2am.

We were all up early the following morning, trying to be the first to pay the bill. This was the way we operated, going out of our way to express the respect we had for one another.

Mark was already at the breakfast table by the time I arrived downstairs. I joined him, then excused myself the first chance I got. I went to pay the bill but Mark had already taken care of it. This was typical of the man. He was the warmest social person you could imagine and interacted with everyone. He had already connected with the owner of the hotel, who insisted on dropping us back to the helicopter.

As soon as we arrived, Damien and I got out but Mark stayed in the car talking to the hotel owner. We understood exactly what was happening. Mark was giving the hotel owner his number, inviting him to Galway and insisting on treating him to dinner in one of his pubs when he came to visit.

While we were waiting for Mark to arrive, Damien phoned Waterford Airport's Air Traffic Control (ATC) before 10am and requested permission to fly from New Ross to the Hook Head area of south Wexford so that we would be able to view the start of the race from the air. But ATC refused to approve the flight plan because of poor visibility and low cloud in that zone. As well as that, they were permitting only one item of traffic into the zone at a time.

We decided to cut our losses and head home. Damien told ATC that he would be taking off shortly anyway and heading west without entering Waterford zone. He subsequently submitted a VFR (visual flight rules) flight plan and a flight time of fifty minutes to Galway.

When Mark finally made it to the helicopter pad, I was sitting in the front seat talking to Damien. I had a lot going on in my head at that time. I was facing court proceedings with my business partners. I wasn't working but had a small fortune tied up in this business. We teased Mark for being late and he casually slipped into the back seat behind me. I said that he should take the front seat but he jokingly insisted that I stay where I was, that being there might ease some of my problems.

It suited Mark that we were leaving early. It was his birthday that Saturday and he would be home in plenty of time to celebrate it with the family he adored. Before we took off, Damien called a friend in Galway who is also a pilot and he told him that the weather was reasonable in the Galway airport area. So off we went in our Robinson R44, a single-piston-engine light helicopter. Its registration was EI-DOC and we called it DOC, after a friend of ours with these initials.

Minutes after take-off Damien signed off with Waterford ATC and transferred to Shannon Airport ATC. The Air Accident Unit report afterwards said that the helicopter was subsequently observed a number of times on Shannon Secondary Surveillance Radar (SSR), initially south-east of Portumna, County Galway. Ten minutes before our anticipated arrival time in Galway, Damien called Shannon and said that he was changing to the Galway frequency. Shannon acknowledged the call and sign-off.

Damien then called Galway ATC but there was no response from Galway, as the duty controller had left the tower for a brief break. Another helicopter on its way to Galway made the last contact with EI-DOC before the crash.

Up to that point, the trip had been pretty uneventful. The thrill of being a front-seat passenger had long worn off me. I was keen to get home. We all were. I remember noticing around 10.40am that we were flying low and close to a mountain. Cloud cover was beginning to restrict our view but we could make out a fleet of steel structures that were reaching up towards us. Ironically, they could have passed for tall ships. I know now that this was the massive wind farm project in Derrybrien in south Galway: seventy-one huge turbine towers, stretching forty-nine metres into the sky, spaced approximately 225 metres apart.

Damien decided to fly into the blanket of cloud. Then he increased our altitude up over the mountain towards the wind farm. It was a judgement call.

At this stage, the cloud cover was not that dense. We were able to see the turbines and Damien manoeuvred the helicopter to ensure that we wouldn't hit any of them. But as we climbed higher, the cloud became thicker. Damien remained calm and collected. He had absolute conviction that we would fly out the other side of the cloud. Mark and I shared that conviction because we trusted him so much.

As we got nearer to the wind farm, the cloud got thicker. The most accurate way to describe it is to think of yourself sitting in the front seat of a car and someone suddenly throwing a white blanket over the windscreen. You can see the dashboard and the windscreen but nothing else. As we flew further into the clouds and closer to the wind farm, the sheer lack of visibility triggered fear and anxiety in us. It's a kind of sick feeling. You are up in the air. You don't know where you are going. You are completely blind. You don't know which way is up or down, left or right. It's disorientation. A sense of complete helplessness.

Damien kept his wits about him. He kept going with the sole intention of flying out the other side of the fog.

If you have ever been in a helicopter, I'm sure it is easy for you to imagine what I am describing. If you haven't and are comparing the experience to being in an aeroplane, think of it as being like descending through cloud cover before the plane lands at an airport. To negotiate your way out of such a situation, you need sophisticated navigational equipment. All we had was a GPS system and a pilot with little flight time.

I don't know how long we were in the fog but I understand that it is quite a common experience for someone who is in a crash or other trauma to lose track of time. As I play it over in my head now, it seems like an hour. Time stands still. It's as if the world has suddenly become an Xbox game and you are going through the levels in slow motion. Every thought is crystal clear. Every vision is in high definition. There is no panic. No screaming. This is real life, not Hollywood. If these were going to be our last moments on this planet, we were going out pumped up on a cocktail of anxiety and adrenaline. All my senses were in overdrive. It was as if I was floating and not really in the cockpit of a helicopter that was about to go down.

It felt like that for a minute or two at most, although at the time it seemed like a lifetime. I can still vividly see the sights, hear the sounds, feel the emotions of that moment. They are stored in my hard-drive. In HD.

Damien must have decided to try to fly back out of the wind farm the way we had flown in. At this stage, no one knew where we were headed. We were blind. Powerless.

We weren't travelling in an automobile. We needed to slow down and turn. Which way? Left or right? The pilot has only seconds to act. Damien decided to reduce speed and take a sharp turn right. The manoeuvre was a shot in the dark. He had no sense of direction. In aviation parlance, it's called spatial disorientation.

As we turned we clipped something. I know now that it was the rotor breaking after hitting a stand of trees. There was no panic. No screaming. I looked at Damien with my mouth open. I knew we were going down.

The helicopter impacted on the northern slopes of the Slieve Aughty Mountains. The crest line of the high ground runs approximately E-W in this area. The helicopter had passed close to the summit, which is 1,174 ft (358 metres) above sea level. This figure does not include the height of the wind turbines located in this area. The helicopter impacted the trees of a dense plantation. At the impact point the terrain is approximately 1,000 ft (305 metres) above sea level, and the taller trees are approx 33 ft (10 metres) high.

The helicopter made initial contact with the trees on a heading of approx 080° at steep angle descent and possibly a high nose down angle. The main rotor blades made progressively heavier contact with the trees, initially with the light tops, but then with the thicker trunks of the trees as it came closer to the ground at this point of major impact. The undercarriage skids separated at this point and the tail rotor assembly departed. Both main rotor blades suffered major damage during this descent through the trees. One main blade spar remained intact, while suffering major distortion. The other blade spar failed approx 0.5 metres from the tip. The separated segment of this blade was not recovered, notwithstanding an extensive air and ground search.

Air Accident Unit Investigation, September 2006

I knew we were finished. We were smashing through a forest at massive speed. The pull of gravity accelerated that speed. It was a real-life horror show. We knew that carnage was imminent, death a strong possibility. People say that your whole life flashes in front of you at moments like this. But my mind was clear. All I

Approx. site of accident

Site of Major Impact

Direction of Flight

Final Position of Helicopter

Initial Impact with Tree Tops

10 07 2005

*Two images from the report of the Air Accident Investigation
Unit, 29 September 2006, showing the site of the accident.*

remember thinking is that we were in serious trouble.

I could see very little. Trees were smashing against the front windscreen. The trees were coming more quickly and becoming denser all the time. It was like watching something in 3D glasses – we were waiting for one of those trees to burst through the screen and take our heads off.

We were waiting for the big bang.

The big smash.

The crash.

The pain. If we were lucky enough to be able to feel pain.

Death.

Through all this pandemonium and chaos, Damien was still struggling with the controls.

'Fuck, fuck, fuck, fuck,' he was saying, in a calm, level voice.

He had no control. We were at the mercy of God and natural forces.

The forward momentum of the helicopter carried the fuselage through a tree. Then we hit the ground with an unmerciful thud. The momentum lessened not one bit. We were sliding through the forest at a crazy, hellish pace.

Everything was in high definition again. There was no panic. Although we were going so fast we were almost in slow motion. We were still conscious and alive. We had to stop somewhere. We had to hit something.

When we did, what awaited us?

An explosion?

Massive trauma?

Death?

Bang.

4

Carnage

It should be noted that the radar plot speed is only the horizontal ground speed component of the helicopter's total speed vector. If the final descent rate was large, which was probably the case, then the airspeed in the final moments of the flight would have been significantly more than the 62 kts plotted ground-speed. This is consistent with the damage suffered by the helicopter.

Air Accident Investigation, September 2006

We hit the ground hard at approximately a hundred and fifteen kilometres (62 knots) an hour. That is not including the force of gravity. That is damn fast and damn hard. No joke.

We came to a juddering halt after hitting two trees. I can clearly remember the moment of impact. I can only describe it as being like a force field slowly coming up through my body. This type of shock is fatal in many cases. It moved up from my toes to my lower spine. I was flung forward with great force. Thankfully, growing up where I did, I had to learn early on how to throw a punch and parry a punch. I reflexively put my arm up to protect my head. The impact smashed my arm and wrist and cracked open my skull but my left arm saved me. If I hadn't had that defensive reaction, I would have been dead or left in a vegetative state.

I was slipping in and out of consciousness. Damien was leaning over me. He was actually more leaning *on* me. Even though it was so obvious, I kept asking Damien what had happened. He replied that we had crashed but that he would get us out of there. He took control of the situation and phoned the emergency services.

We were in no-man's land. A hellhole on the side of a mountain. I wasn't aware that full coverage is available all over Ireland for 999 emergency calls. Damien and I had two different service providers and when his call dropped because of patchy coverage, he had the presence of mind to ask for my phone and return the call to the emergency services. Despite his serious injuries, Damien had the survival instinct to give the emergency services as good an idea of our position as he could. We were in the middle of a forest, in rough terrain, beside a wind farm.

You might think that a helicopter crash in surroundings such as these would leave a devastating trail of destruction, an instant map and set of coordinates for rescuers. But this was not the case. Our helicopter, a Robinson R44, nicknamed the black widow in the aviation industry, was small, with a tiny cabin. It would have left little or no visible imprint of where we had gone down. We hit about thirty trees before we crashed but this was like clipping a few hairs off a thick mane. The point where the main rotor blades first made contact with the tree tops was not distinguishable from the air because the plantation was so dense. Ground-based emergency services were also bound to be hampered in their efforts to locate the accident site by the absence of an accurate position fix and by the fact that the terrain was so mountainous.

Although my mind was all over the place I knew it would be difficult for the rescue services to find us and I wasn't sure how long it would take, so any time I regained consciousness, I tried to get out of the helicopter. There was no way I would have been able to move and Damien kept telling me to stay put but my instinct was to get the hell out of the wreckage. I was afraid we would go up in flames. We were carrying a significant amount of fuel but landing in marshy soil had reduced the possibility of that apocalyptic ending.

Damien was a member of the helicopter club in Galway and very popular there. Once word went out that he had crashed, a number of pilots took to the skies to help in the rescue operation. By now, the coastguard Sikorsky S61 helicopter had been summoned. Once this happens, all other pilots are instructed to vacate the airspace. One helicopter pilot refused to do so. Later on he was reprimanded for failing to follow protocol but sometimes you have to risk getting into trouble to do the right thing. He continued to hover over the crash area in a desperate bid to locate the site. Although it was nearly impossible given the density of the forest, he eventually spotted us. He landed his helicopter on a roadway about a hundred metres from the accident site and gave the location directions to the ground rescue services. The Garda sergeant who headed up the ground search told me later that if we had not been found pretty soon the army would have been called in.

The improvement in the weather between the time of the accident and the arrival of the first helicopter on the scene was critical in the location of the accident site. At that time, about 11.15am, the cloud base was approximately 1500 feet above sea level or about 300 feet above the high ground. When the S61 arrived shortly afterwards, it took over aerial command of the situation.

To get to us, the ground rescue services had to battle their way through a thicket of scrub and bushes. I remember hearing someone shouting and Damien shouting back to alert them to our location. When they arrived, they took Damien out first, although he protested that he should be left to last. When they cut me out, at first they thought I didn't recognise them. They asked me questions as if they were conducting a cognitive test but I knew exactly who they were. I knew they had come to try to save us.

After being given preliminary treatment, I was slipped into a harness and winched up to the S61, which was hovering overhead. Even that was a surreal feeling. I clearly remember the force of being pulled skywards, which reminded me of the force I experienced when we crashed. It's the reason I will never go near motorbikes, jet skis or – obviously – helicopters ever again.

> Given the speed of impact, the high deceleration caused by the final impact with tree trunks, and the light construction of the cabin of the helicopter, survival was unlikely. The compaction of the rear seat area, in particular, made survival in this area improbable.
>
> Air Accident Investigation, September 2006

I don't remember Mark being winched up but I think he was already in the helicopter by the time I was pulled in. He had suffered major injuries and had not responded to the efforts of the emergency services to revive him. I didn't ask about him. My instinct was that he was already dead. I was right.

When Damien was hauled in, I asked him what had happened. 'What do you think happened!' was his reply. Even at this moment of crisis and tragedy, Damien's dry wit had not deserted him. These were the last words I spoke to him.

By now, the word was out. Hyland, a friend of Damien, had been frantically trying to get someone to meet us at the heli-pad at University College Hospital, Galway. John Mannion, Mark's business partner and a friend to us all, was on his way to the crash site when he got a call to tell him to turn back and head for UCHG. He was at the heli-pad when we landed. Mark was taken out first. It was clear that he was in a very bad way. I can still see the distress on John's face when he spotted Mark.

When Damien was lifted out, he raised his eyes to heaven in a very characteristic way, as if to underline how much trouble we were in. He never lost his character and grit.

I have always been a fighter. I had a moment of clarity as soon as we landed and said to myself that I had no intention of being removed from the aircraft on a stretcher. It was a ludicrous idea, evidence of my stubborn streak. I was alive, against all the odds for a helicopter crash. I had cheated death. It was as if I was trying to prove a point.

As I was being taken out, I saw John Mannion. 'Howya,' I said to him.

The doctors had already asked John who my next of kin was, so John said to me, 'Mike, what's your sister's number?'

I fired Karen's number straight at him but I left out one digit, which meant they couldn't contact her. I was sitting up on the stretcher, as if I didn't want to look weak by lying on my back, which was broken almost in two. John later told me that I looked like someone who was heading for a party somewhere.

There was no party.

The music was over.

They were still trying to resuscitate Mark but he was already dead. That should have been me.

Damien died a few hours later.

When I reflect on it now, I feel I am alive because of one decision, the selfless, kind gesture of a friend. It should have been me in the back of that helicopter, not Mark, but he knew I had a lot on my mind. It was just a small thing but it was his way of trying to help appease my worries. It summed up Mark's kind nature. He saved my life.

I have often thought about that since the day of the crash. Not the fact that I survived a helicopter crash but Mark's selflessness. If Mark hadn't been so thoughtful, I wouldn't be here now.

That's the beauty of life. You never know what is around the corner. You can stress about life all you want but much of it is totally outside your control. Many people have said to me that

I survived because 'my time was not up'. Really it was a way for them to attempt to make sense of a complete mystery like death. At first I did not like hearing the phrase. After the accident, I didn't spent much time thinking about things like that. I was too busy getting my life back. But I came around to this way of thinking and as I reflect on it all years later, it makes more and more sense.

The truth is that no one knows why one person dies and another survives. It could be down to anything. Karma. Fate. Sheer luck. I just accept it for what it is and move on. That way I won't get stuck in the past. For me, the past tense is never an option.

Before we left Wexford that morning, the three of us were on top of the world. Within an hour, we were in a living hell. That's how quickly everything can change and be turned upside down. That's why you have to live life to the absolute maximum. Chase your dreams. Fulfil your potential. Avoid the negative at all costs. The end can come at any time. Whatever our dreams are, we all want to 'do it' but unfortunately, for whatever reason, not everyone gets around to 'doing it'. My two friends 'did it'. The least you owe yourself is to attempt to 'do it'.

That weekend, we had one spot left in the helicopter for the trip to Waterford. For a bit of fun, we tried get someone to fill it and approached all the usual suspects: Mannion, Hyland, Harlowe, Farragher. Maybe one or two more. John Mannion was the one who should have been on that trip with us. He had more or less committed to going when a Garda inspection of his pub was announced for that Saturday morning and he had no choice but to cancel. We had lunch in the Front Door the afternoon before we left and we met John and asked him again if there was any chance he could join us. I knew he was disappointed to miss out on the trip but that Garda inspection probably saved his life.

Half of Galway claimed to be the person who was due to take

the last seat on the day of the accident. It got so bad that my aunt told me she felt like screaming, she heard about so many people who were 'supposed to be in that seat'. Other stories circulated as to what really happened. There were maybe a thousand different theories as to why we crashed. But the only one who knows is me.

Details emerged at the coroner's court that were very helpful. The head of the flying club where the helicopter was stationed made statements that really grabbed our attention. He was a very experienced pilot and an excellent speaker and left no one present in any doubt about the validity of his testimony. He explained in detail that a helicopter is not like a car. You cannot press a brake and come to a dead stop. As the helicopter is in the air the pilot needs to reduce speed. Then, when the aircraft is at a reasonable speed, the pilot makes a manoeuvre, either right or left, up or down. Or he can choose to turn around.

It could be argued that this is what Damien attempted to do but it is not true. He was flying through the fog, trying to get out the other side.

Another friend was with Mark and me when we had a conversation with Damien about the perils of flying a helicopter and he also remembers the conversation. Particularly as Damien was a relatively inexperienced pilot, we were all curious as to what could happen to us as passengers on the helicopter.

I can still recall the questions we posed, which Damien answered very decisively.

What if the engine failed?

You train how to emergency-land a helicopter with engine failure.

It sounded risky but Damien was one of the most confident people we knew and we trusted him a hundred per cent.

What happens if you fly into fog? (That's certainly a legitimate question to ask in Ireland.)

That's simple. If you fly into fog, you fly out the other side.

That's what Damien tried to do that day but it didn't work out the way he hoped. Damien was the calmest and most relaxed person you could ever meet. I owe my life to the bravery he showed after the crash when he selflessly tried to help Mark and me first, with no regard for himself. Of course he could, as a pilot, have made different decisions. But that's true anywhere you turn in life. You make decisions in the moment. You can't take all the possible consequences into consideration in advance when you have only a moment to decide.

Not long before we crashed, we crossed a significant road, the R352. Had Damien followed that road north, then followed the R351 (the Woodford-Loughrea road), we would have reached Loughrea, then on to Galway via the N6. By taking this route he would have avoided the high ground of Slieve Aughty.

I don't doubt Damien for a second. He took the route he felt was best. Without his prompt actions the day of the crash I would probably not have survived or, if I had, I mightn't have recovered as well as I did from my injuries. My injuries were so severe that I could have died if we had been trapped in that mangled wreck for a long time. When I was desperately trying to move, he forcefully instructed me not to. In hindsight, knowing I had a burst L3 vertebra in my back, I am thankful that I took his advice. Otherwise my life would be very different today.

Damien saved my life but he couldn't save his own. He had suffered critical internal injuries, primarily caused by the seat belt. He underwent an operation in hospital that day to stem the bleeding but it was unsuccessful. He died at 10pm.

We set off from Wexford that day, our lives full of promise and excitement. We felt we were untouchable, invulnerable. It was almost as if nature had smeared the word 'Vulnerable' across the mangled wreckage on the side of a mountain.

5

Mother and Sister

Karen Brown

I'll never forget how I found out. My husband Phil was meeting my sister's husband Niall in Sheridan's, Mark's pub in Knocknacarra. It had been on the news that a helicopter had come down. Phil was calling a second pint when a call came through behind the bar and all of a sudden the barman said, 'Sorry lads, I have to close.' It immediately clicked with Phil and he asked the barman if it had something to do with the helicopter crash. The barman said, 'I can't say anything.' Phil said that his brother-in-law was in that helicopter so the barman came clean. 'The helicopter has come down,' he said. 'And I don't know if they are dead or alive.'

Phil got straight into the car. He rang me and said, 'Have the door unlocked.' I didn't know what he was talking about. A minute later he drove in the driveway and I thought he was going to come in through the kitchen window. He ran in and asked, 'Where's your mother?'

He was shaking and I said, 'Have you knocked someone down or what?

He asked my mother and me to sit down. He told us not to panic but that the helicopter had crashed.

It was pure pandemonium. We didn't know what to do. We rang the hospital. They said that they were due to come in but they couldn't give us any information. They told us to ring Gort garda station. We did. The only information they could give us what that there was one fatality. But they couldn't say who.

It was horrifying. We were out of our minds with worry.

After someone rang my other sister to break the news, I phoned the hospital again. I spoke to a nurse.

'He is here,' she said. 'He is critical but he is alive.'

We were concerned about Norrie, my other sister, as she had just had a baby. She had no adult with her out in Clifden, about an hour from Galway, and she had to drive in with Rachel, her little girl. We were afraid something might happen to her. So a nurse talked to her on the phone to try to calm her down.

By the time we arrived at the hospital, there must have been nearly a thousand people there. The word was out by then and the whole town seemed to be converging on the place. They were all standing around in small groups. They kept looking at us, then putting their heads down.

We were brought in. Mark was dead by that stage. I remember seeing Damien in a room before he was brought in for surgery. Then Mike was wheeled out in a trolley. He was in terrible pain with his back and he kept asking, 'Where are the lads? Where are they?'

Carmel Gibbons

On the way over to the hospital, I was out of my mind. I kept saying, 'My Mikey, my Mikey.'

I said to myself, 'He has to be dead. He has to be dead.' I mean how could you fall out of the sky and not be dead? To me, helicopters are like flying motorbikes. I thought, 'That's it, he must be gone.' I had a feeling the hospital might not be telling us the full truth about the number of people who were dead.

Karen Brown

The doctors were looking for Mike's mobile to contact Stella, his girlfriend, who was in America at the time, as well as Damien's girlfriend, who was also in America.

When I opened Mike's bag to get the mobile, his denim jacket was inside. It clicked with me then that this was why people wouldn't look at us when we were on our way into the hospital. They thought it was Mike who was dead.

Carmel Gibbons

They were letting people into the hospital. Mark's family members were there. His friends were there. They were all around him. It was terrible. Heartbreaking.

We still didn't know what the story was with Mikey. We knew he was alive but we didn't know how bad he was. Next thing he was wheeled out on a trolley.

I went over to him. He opened his eyes and said, 'Hi Mam.'

I knew he was alive but I went to a doctor and asked, 'Is he going to die? '

The doctor said, 'I think he is going to live, he is the least injured.'

He was in desperate pain. I knew he was in huge trouble with his back. I had this terrible feeling that he would never walk again. Knowing Mikey, I thought that nothing would hit him harder that not being able to walk.

Karen Brown

We were told not to say anything. Shane McInerney, Mike's friend, who was a doctor in the hospital, had told us not to say anything. 'I know Mike,' he said. 'I know he is going to push you and push you for answers but you cannot tell him Mark is dead. He is critical and he could go into shock if you tell him.'

When I went into his room he kept asking. I said, 'I think they are fine. I think they will be all right.'

He was staring at me, staring through me. He knew.

By this stage, I was in a state. I was six months pregnant and they began monitoring my blood pressure to make sure I was OK. A couple of hours later, after Mike had been brought up to the intensive care unit, I went for a walk. I knew Damien had been in surgery and I happened to meet John Mannion. I asked him if Damien was out of surgery yet.

I will never forget his look. He said to me, 'Did you not hear?'

That was when my knees gave way. I collapsed.

Carmel Gibbons

I knew Mark was dead. Then when I heard that Damien had died, I said to myself, 'Even if Mikey survives, how is he going to live now? He couldn't possibly live a normal life.' After losing his two best friends, I thought there would be some devastating mental side-effects. Even if he was able to walk, he could not make a full recovery. I thought he would never walk again. I could see him in a wheelchair for the rest of my life.

Karen Brown

Later on, I wanted to go in to Mikey but he refused to see me. He refused all of us point blank. He knew then that the lads were dead. I went to Shane again and I said, 'This is not going to work, we have to make a decision.' We went home and I spoke to Ronan, Mike's best friend, and he agreed with me. We felt that not being told would have a worse effect on him. We agreed then that Ronan would come in with me the following morning to tell him.

When we told him the next morning, he said, 'I already know.'

6

Pain

I was in pain. Severe pain. It was grinding into my bones, ripping through every sinew of my body. My muscles were screaming. And then the morphine drip was inserted into my bloodstream and the respite came in calm waves. As long as I could push that button to release more morphine into my aching body, everything was OK.

I still had enough energy to talk to my family, who were there by my side. I knew I could rely on them for anything but I have a stubborn streak and had no real intention of depending on anyone. I wanted to know one thing: how were Mark and Damien? It must have been the way my mother and sisters were talking around the subject that triggered my relentless pursuit of the answers. Any time I asked about them, they would almost look away from me, avoiding eye contact. In all honesty, that told me everything. I sensed that the lads were both dead but I wanted confirmation.

I had suffered serious injuries, including brain injury. It is only natural that medical personnel would not want to cause any more mental distress in a patient already in serious physical distress. This would be normal protocol for someone who was in my situation. But doctors don't know everything. Medically, they are excellent guides, with all their years of training and experience. But you have to deal with every individual differently, especially someone who is in the middle of the storm. If you know them, you will know the right time to break bad news.

My doctors advised my family to gather all my closest friends in a show of support before delivering the harrowing information. But I completely raged against this scenario. It may have been the most desirable one in the eyes of the doctors but it was the wrong option for someone with my type of personality.

I didn't want to be crowded. I didn't want to be shrouded in pity or draped in condolences. I wanted it in black and white. Give me the facts and I would deal with them. People sometimes think that because you have been seriously injured you somehow lose your personality. They are afraid that you are not the same person, that an unspeakable tragedy has taken your soul and replaced it with a ghost.

Psychologists, psychiatrists and medical personnel have their own theories about how best to deal with a situation like the one I was in – but you must know the personality of the patient. If you do, you will know better than anyone how to break bad news to them. Don't rely on doctors to tell you. Read the situation yourself.

That might sound like a rage against medical convention and science but I can only speak from my own experience. After I was told, I faced my own traumatic episode. With the passage of time I realise that it was my survival personality taking control of the situation. I had to deal with the new reality straight away. Everyone has a different personality but every personality is hard-wired to survive, no matter what anyone says. It is innate. It is a matter of activating it.

I am often asked about survivor guilt. About depression. About post-traumatic stress disorder (PTSD). People are familiar with this term from the media without really understanding it. They assume that you begin to experience symptoms – depression, guilt, anger and panic attacks – straight after such a horrendous accident and that it leads to long-term deterioration in your mental health. In other words, that you are on the road to nowhere.

Nothing could be further from the truth. You don't wake up one morning with PTSD. Survivor guilt doesn't suddenly kick in. Depression doesn't immediately ransack your senses and seize control of your life. These effects come on you gradually and you may face them repeatedly in different ways. But once you get over the initial trauma, you can condition yourself to deal with whatever darkness is lurking around the corner. Your survival personality will take care of the rest.

When it was confirmed to me that my friends were dead, I asked everyone to leave the room. Then I called the nurse in and told her that I did not want to see anyone.

'Anyone except your family,' she replied.

'No one.'

I needed time on my own. I had to get some head space to work through the debris, to try to figure all this out.

I rebooted my system. I thought back to what had happened. I could remember 80 per cent of the events of the previous day. My body was broken and battered by injuries. My friends were dead. What did the future hold? It seemed overwhelming. I lay in the bed and tried to scream but no sound came. I may have been heavily medicated but I had a profound sense of clarity at that moment, a clarity that was coursing through every part of me. In that intense moment I was possessed by a spirit of acceptance. Acceptance that my friends were dead but I was alive. And I knew immediately that I would get through this.

I have no idea how I long I was in this state of mind but the feeling was so strong that I knew I had nailed it. The confidence I felt had already begun to ease the pain. The sense of acceptance I had was the best morphine you could ever ask for.

When the tide is on top of you, you can't row against it. The harder you try the more it will engulf you. There were rough seas ahead now but my survival personality would provide me with the boat, oars and compass to negotiate my way through the stormy waves.

Maybe it is easy for me to talk about a survival personality. Maybe I had the luxury of always being able to draw on such an asset. Maybe it was easier for me to activate it because my mother had always taught me to think rationally, to accept things for what they were, then move on. Anyone who knows me knows that I don't mess around. If something needs to be done, I do it.

But it would have been easy for me, lying in that hospital room, to be paralysed by fear and guilt and recriminations. I had crashed into the side of a mountain. My friends were dead. For all I knew at that stage, I could have been facing a compromised life because of my injuries. Would that life be worth living? Would I be better off if the crash had taken me too?

The demons are always looking for a place to squat. If you let them in the door, they'll colonise your whole head. And if that happens, you may as well hand over the keys and let them wreck the rest of your life. I wasn't letting them inside the door. They could squat somewhere else. To ensure they didn't try come back again later, when the medication had worn off and the pain was knifing through my body, I barricaded the door to my mind with steel. I piled up the barriers, one by one.

I had played no part in the events that led to the crash and it wasn't going to beat me. There was no point wondering what might have happened. It had happened. I had been hit hard. I could have let it beat me to my knees and keep me there permanently. I could have spent the rest of my days languishing in regret and remorse. I had no intention of doing so. I had already begun the process of moving forward.

There was no point in being consumed by the events that had happened. I needed to embrace them and let the memories of the accident and the death of my friends become part of my new life.

This is what I did.

I knew the pain wasn't going anywhere anytime soon. It was there to torment me, to eat into me like a virus. The morphine alleviated the aches that were thumping my body like a jackhammer but drugs were only ever going to do so much. It's like being in a haze that you feel will never lift.

At one stage, Shane McInerney, a doctor in the hospital and a good friend of mine, came into the room. He had his white coat on and his stethoscope around his neck and a serious look in his eyes. Mac certainly wasn't arriving in for a chat about what had gone down the night before in Halo, the local nightclub.

My sister Karen approached him. Her face was creased with anxiety and worry. She whispered something in Shane's ear. I couldn't hear what she said but I knew a couple of seconds later. He walked to the bottom of the bed, peeled back the sheets and began to tickle my feet. Instantly, I started wiggling my toes.

I knew I would walk again but the pain in my back was intense. Pain is a battle most of us face at one time or another and we have a simple choice in this battle. We either accept this pain or we fight it.

Of course pain is physical but often it can be as much mental as physical. It's really a fight in your brain, a battle between reality and the unknown. Like the demons of PTSD it is a bunch of gremlins invading your mind. They talk to you, they can infiltrate your thought processes and they are constantly sending you messages like these:

This pain is never going to go away.
This is with you for life.
If anything, this pain is going to get worse.
The pain is so bad that you might never be able to walk again.
In other words, you're finished.

The pain gremlins were trying to torture me in the hours after the crash, to drive the knife into my gut and twist it into my spine.

The pain was so intense it felt inhuman. I saw black dots. I felt ready to faint on many occasions. But my spirit was never going to collapse from an explosion of negativity inside my head.

I removed the focus from the negativity in my brain and stored it somewhere in the back of my head. In other words, I compartmentalised it. This might sound trivial, as if I was putting an old jacket away in the attic. But that is effectively where I was putting it – in the attic of my mind. I was not going to be beaten. I refused to let it get the better of me. I refused to concede defeat in my head. That is really where the battle is won. You must overcome the pain in your brain.

It's funny how life repeats itself. A few years after the accident, I had a lump on my chest and my doctor sent me to see a specialist. When I met the surgeon, he took one look at my file. Then he shook his head. He asked me if I knew him. I said I didn't. He gave me a clue. I still hadn't any idea. He could have been the Pope for all I knew. But when he told me that I had made a remarkable recovery, I began to get the picture.

The hospital in Galway had an emergency plan that is activated in serious accidents where casualty numbers are unknown. Our crash activated this emergency plan. The man standing in front of me now was the chief surgeon on duty on the day of the accident It was he who had operated on Damien. He told me that he felt he would have been able to save Damien's life if he had operated on him earlier.

I didn't believe that to be the case. When you are seriously injured, as Damien was, you need to fight. You need the warrior in you to come out and battle hard. You have to decide in your own head that this cannot beat you.

Deep down, I know that Damien gave up. He knew that Mark was already dead. For all I know, he could have thought that the same fate was awaiting me. And I know what Damien would have been thinking. He wouldn't have been able to live with himself.

Damien was never one to walk away from a fight but, in his own head, this was one fight too many.

When Damien was in college, it was difficult to get anyone to enter into a round of drinks with him. He was a huge man and there was no point trying to match him round for round. It would be a knockout, with Damien standing over you as you lay on the canvas.

This was something I found hard to understand. Was this drinking concealing some demon he didn't want to face? I suspected that he suffered from depression. There were plenty of times when the darkness appeared to be enveloping him. I would look at him and worry. The dark cloud would almost paralyse his personality, something that didn't suit a man who always wanted to be free in spirit.

I knew that there had to be something more to it. That dark cloud had to have an origin. I once heard a throwaway remark about a accident Damien had once been involved in. Someone had passed away. That was as much as I knew and I didn't pursue the subject. It was none of my business.

Although we spent lots of time together, Damien brought this topic up only once. Shortly before we travelled to Australia in 2004, we were in a pub one night shooting the breeze. We were both in great form, even laughing at the possibility that both of us could be out of work by the time we returned from Australia.

Drink obviously loosened Damien's tongue and overcame his inhibitions. He told me that he had been in an accident a few years earlier, that he had been driving and that a passenger had been killed.

I was taken aback. I enquired how he was mentally and he said he was fine. It is only when I looked back on the conversation after the accident that I realised my ignorance in asking the question. I made an assumption, just as so many people have made an assumption about my mental state since the accident.

We never spoke about it again until we were in Australia, when, one night. Damien told me the full story. He went out for a spin in a car with another guy, the car crashed and his young passenger lost his life.

Damien had made a great go of his life. His success was a testament to his willpower and drive and motivation. Yet the guilt of that event had never left him. He blamed himself entirely.

I then understood what was behind the dark cloud I had often wondered about. A professional once said something chilling to me: 'If I had that hanging over me, I would drink myself to sleep every night as well.' Although everything appeared to be going so well for Damien, he was carrying an enormous burden of guilt. The loss of a second human life, or even two human lives, would have been unbearable.

Damien would not have been able to live with the guilt of having killed someone else. For all he knew, the deaths of two people could have been hanging over him for the rest of his life. An ocean of beer would not have been enough to drown that level of remorse.

Losing the fight, the battle, was unlike Damien. He had a heart of gold and the personality of a lion but I fully understood why he gave up. John Mannion said to me that he could see the disappointment and devastation on Damien's face that day as he was being lifted out of the Air Rescue helicopter. That regret was possibly worse than any pain that was ripping through his body. Damien died on the operating table later that evening. But he was already dead before he was put on the table.

It was different for me. I wasn't racked by guilt or remorse and I had no intention of backing down from the fight. I had no idea where life was going to take me but it certainly wasn't going to bring me to my knees and keep me there. The pain was appalling but it was only going to last for so long. I was going to get up. I was going to live.

Two lives had ended the previous day. Two wonderful journeys had come to an end. But my journey was only beginning.

7

People

You have to have lived in New York City to fully appreciate that it really is the city that never sleeps. The attitude of the place is amazing. The pace is hectic. The speed is relentless. There isn't even a snooze button to press.

New Yorkers don't have time to slow down. Rest is rust. New Yorkers seem to live in a parallel world to the rest of mankind. When have you ever met anyone who has come to NY for an average job? It doesn't happen. New Yorkers want the best. They demand it. On the other hand, do New Yorkers know that another world exists outside their bubble? Are New Yorkers moving at such a pace that they are often, effectively, sleepwalking?

It is fascinating to watch people. On occasion, I have seen visitors lost in the city ask local people for directions. New Yorkers are startled when that happens. You might be too if you were hustled out of your own mental zone and into the outside world. It is written all over their faces. Firstly, they are half-shocked that someone has intruded into their little world. Then you see the wheels turning in their heads, whirring them back to reality and humanity. These individuals who would walk all over you if you fell under their feet at rush hour suddenly become caring human beings. Having returned to reality, they often go out of their way to be helpful.

Perhaps I am being unfair to New Yorkers. Most of us have the same mentality. We are in a little bubble and things outside that bubble don't matter all that much. It often takes something extraordinary for us to break out of the bubble and see the bigger picture. Although people are mostly good by nature, they live their own lives. One thing that is true of people everywhere is that, when disaster strikes, they can be extraordinary in their response. They display remarkable kindness and generosity. They go above and beyond the call of duty. But you can almost predict the pattern. Something terrible happens to someone and another person has a certain reaction but really it is almost like a chemical reaction, a kind of vapour release of emotion, that will spread only so far and last for so long. In truth, a quick fix.

Here is an analogy. Think of having a long-lost relative come to visit you. Initially you treat them like royalty. You serve them the best food you can cook. You put new sheets on the bed to make their stay even more comfortable. You wrap them in kindness at every turn. But after a couple of days of making a fuss, you want them gone.

When it comes to a tragedy you can condense people's attention to a few hours or even a few minutes. It is only natural that, after the initial drama and the compassion they feel as a result, people want a return to their own lives. It is your life that has changed as a result of an accident, not theirs. You have to get used to a new reality, while their reality stays the same. They don't want any awkward feelings towards you or about you to intrude into their reality.

No matter how much you dress it up people love to feel sorry for a victim. Especially in the west of Ireland. It's so obvious that you can almost hear the violins and the sad music playing when you see people approaching you. You can almost hear what they're thinking.

The poor unfortunate.

Jeez, that poor old devil might never walk again.

God love his poor mother and sisters, they will have to deal with

that basket case now for the rest of their lives.
He will never be right again.
I'm telling you, he will be racked with guilt.
Depression will tear him apart.
It will make him even more screwed up in the head.
He will probably even take his own life after a while.

When these people approach me, I can spot them and their thoughts a mile off and what I'm thinking is: 'Will you ever clear off and unload your fabricated compassion and warped perspective somewhere else.'

This is not true of everyone but it is often what you discover when you are recovering from a serious accident. A dramatic event brings them all out from under the rocks. People I had been to school with but hadn't seen in years made contact with me. Half-friends and old acquaintances I no longer had any connection with were beating down the door to see me.

Why were these people contacting me now? Where were they for years? I know everyone's life gets busier as we get older and it's natural that ties are cut. But reconnecting with someone after a serious accident is often a link so false and thin that you could cut it with your fingers.

People often want to feel better about themselves by feeling sorry for the victim. Life is tough. When they see someone who has had it tougher, they are instinctively thankful that they are not that person. Because it would not be acceptable to express this feeling, they 'console' the victim by telling them things could be worse.

It could be worse.
You could be in heaven like Mark and Damien.
You still have people around you who love you.
We will be here for you, no matter what.

The last one is a classic. Really? When will you be around? To give me the help I need every day while I'm incapacitated?

Of course I don't want you around. Of course you won't be around. So why say it?

I believe people say things like this to make themselves feel better; it has nothing to do with person who's had the accident.

The other side of the coin is that Irish people are the best-natured and kindest people on the planet. What Hugh Leonard wrote is probably an accurate description: 'An Irishman will always soften bad news, so that a major coronary is no more than "a bad turn". And a near hurricane that leaves thousands homeless is "good drying weather".'

There were plenty of people who visited me in hospital, people I hadn't seen in ages, who really picked me up. I was as high as a kite on morphine and the fun really started when I was moved into a new ward. So many people and so much fun. So many stories. Despite the tragedy of having lost my two great friends, I still had my sense of humour. This is the great thing about being Irish. Believe me, when the darkness descends, you are in trouble if you don't have a sense of humour. Visits from those people provided very welcome respite in the early days. The reason we had such fun was that they didn't treat me as a victim. They didn't project their sympathy or remorse on to me. They treated me as normal. And I responded to it.

In the days after the accident, although I knew I had the support of my family and close friends I was also aware that I was alone in this. It was all up to me. If I had been married with children, would it have been any different? I don't think so. No matter how much support you receive, your recovery is really up to yourself.

I have no interest in sport but I have a good friend who is a sports fanatic. He told me about Bill Belichick, coach to the renowned New England Patriots football team. A few hours before the Patriots took the field at one of the three Superbowls they won in four years, Belichick made a speech at a team meeting.

American football is the most technical, tactical and pre-planned sport on the planet but on this particular day, Belichick brought it all back down to one simple mantra: 'Do your job.'

Despite the myriad game plans the coaches had drawn up that players had to execute, the routes they had to run, tackles they had to make, kicks they had to nail, plays they had to call, injuries they had to sort out on the hoof, everyone in the organisation had one simple priority to focus on – do your job. Nothing else– the razzmatazz, hype, huge crowds, the bonus money, the MVP award – none of it mattered. Once the game began, all that counted was that everyone did their job.

That was what it was going to come down to for me. I had a job to do. Doctors, nurses, family and friends were going to help me to do that job. But no one but myself could do it. My job was to recover and I was going to do it.

Another issue came to the surface before long. I don't know if this is true of other countries but in Ireland, sympathy often lasts for only a few weeks. Then the half-truths and rumour take hold. Irish people have theories about everything and love to be the ones with the inside story. Although we may not admit it, we love to be the one with the real scoop on the victim.

Westside, where I grew up in Galway, was initially regarded as a rough neighbourhood. It matured into a really good area in time but it never lost that sense of community that hardship fostered. The saying on the street was always the same: 'If you are in distress or unsure, the best policy is to say nothing.' In the days immediately after the accident, I swung from chronic pain to mental torture to morphine-induced euphoria. There was not much I could know for sure but my primary instinct was to say nothing.

My priority was to protect Damien's good name. I had a good sense of what had happened in the accident but I was hearing all sorts of rumours that had no basis in reality. One guy in particular seemed to be dining out on the attention he was getting from reportedly being in the know.

No matter where you turned, you heard a different story, such as the report that I nearly drowned after the crash, that the helicopter came down in bog water and that my head was submerged. Someone spread another story that my lungs were full of bog water when they rescued me. That kind of nonsense.

My sister Karen was home from Wales one weekend and she and I went out for a drink. We went into town and the amount of rubbernecking that went on was ridiculous. We could hear all the whispering going on around us. 'There's your man who survived the crash. There he is.'

We went into a pub and a person came up and asked me how I was. I said I was fine and the person said, 'But how are you really? How are you mentally? Sure you couldn't be normal.' The pressure was continuous. I couldn't even have five minutes to be myself. We hopped into a taxi and came straight home – we couldn't cope with it.'

A while back – a long time after the accident – I met my oldest friend, Jimmy, for a few drinks in Galway one evening. I spotted a guy I had been in school with. He beat a path in my direction, with a look of shock and horror on his face.

'Jesus, you are alive!' he shouted, as if Lazarus has appeared before him. 'Get this man a drink.'

It was as if he was celebrating a resurrection. I remember thinking, 'Not the helicopter crash again.'

Apparently, he had been playing poker with someone from Galway. My name came up and he was reliably informed that I had gone to the US and died of cancer.

It didn't surprise me. This was the latest of a long list of misfortunes that had befallen me since the helicopter came down.

It's easy to see the logic behind all this. My friends were dead. Most people couldn't see how I could be right after such a traumatic event. It was as if I had also died that day, so people made up their own minds, or their own stories, as to how I had gone about dying.

After a disaster, you can never escape being perceived as a victim. It is like a tattoo that can't be removed by laser surgery. No matter what else you do in life, you will always be that victim.

At that stage of my life – December 2012 – I had a degree from Columbia University. But I found myself wondering if I should really have that life. I was probably projecting this from how I thought other people perceived me.

When I was feeling low and sorry for myself I found myself believing that people would have preferred to see me beat up and broken down or seeking answers at the bottom of a bottle rather than trying to better myself. This would somehow have made them feel better about their own lives – otherwise why would they have been like this? I felt that these energy vampires were everywhere, that they were sucking the life out of me. Although this was too much of a generalisation it made me feel bitter at a time when life was very hard for me.

I know now I generalised too much about people. The majority of people are kind-hearted and good-natured and wanted the best for me. But after my accident, I was often angry and frustrated, something that coloured my view of people and how they reacted to me. I was wrong to judge people harshly. But this judgement may have helped to keep me strong, strong enough to focus on my recovery and resist having other people shape my destiny.

8

Steps

Do you ever watch those Discovery Channel programmes about lions and tigers on the Serengeti plains? These animals need to hunt to stay alive. When they isolate their prey, they chase it down. Nothing is going to stop them. A gazelle hasn't a hope in hell. I won't go as far as to say I am a tiger. But that is often how I view my life. I need to be busy. To chase down life. In the days after the accident, I felt like a caged tiger on the Serengeti. I couldn't hunt and I needed to hunt to stay alive.

I was sick of people feeling sorry for me. That form of sympathy is like a virus. It eats away at your soul. People mean well but after a while it's almost as if you are carrying this huge container of pity around on your back. All I wanted to do was to throw that container out the window.

I wanted to help myself. I needed to help myself. How could I do that in my physical state? I needed to get back to doing things that I liked doing. After such a serious accident, it is inevitable that normality becomes secondary to the routines and procedures of hospital. I needed normality, not to be weighed down by medical jargon or the physical and mental implications of what the future would hold. To shape my own future, I had to take control back from the hospital.

The first step was paramount. I set myself a tiny goal. It was my number one priority. I was going to get of bed. I kept saying it to people but they ignored me. This is normal after such an accident.

People want the best for you. Of course getting out of bed is not advisable for someone who has broken his back. It would be reckless for someone close to you to facilitate your wishes.

But I was being treated as a victim. I wasn't a victim. I didn't feel like one. I didn't want to be one. So to counter all those perceptions of me as a poor, injured victim I had to get out of bed. It might be no more than one or two small steps but it would be one or two small steps further away from the pool of sympathy that I was drowning in.

My mother claims she is not a smart person but she is wise as well as modest. At one stage, we were alone in the room together and I asked her what I was going to do. She told me that I would be all right. And I knew it too.

Later she said, 'There was nothing special about what I said to Mikey that day. I said, "You are down as low as you can go. You can only go up now. You are strong-minded. We will come through this." I'm sure I also said to him, "You are thick as a ditch, like you always were, you will be fine." He never had a father. He went to school but he always said, "It's some education being raised by three wise women."'

I accepted early in life that women are smarter than us men.

My mother was right. I was low but the only way to go was up. Now it was basically about choosing my attitude. If I wanted to feel sorry for myself, I had every ready-made excuse imaginable. No one would have said a word to me or thought any the worse of me if I had opted to take that route. But it was never an option.

I had to look at everything clinically. Bad luck was really what caused the accident so there was no point in making more of it than it really was. My mother said something to me that day that really stuck, that my bad luck would turn to good luck but that I should never forget the bad luck because when my good luck did return, it would make me appreciate it all the more.

A few days after the accident, I had to be transferred to Merlin

Park hospital to have my arm pinned. The bone in my left arm was shattered and I spent six hours in surgery. I now have a plate running from my elbow to my wrist. But that was the least of my worries at that time. When I was moved for the operation I was still lying on a spinal board because they didn't know the full extent of my back injuries. To make matters worse, the media circus tailed me across town. Reporters were camped outside the hospital door trying to get at me to drill me for information. In Galway, this was a big story and I was the only one still around to tell it.

I shut all that out of my mind. I had one goal – to walk as soon as I could. The doctors were still observing my progress but I felt that I needed to accelerate the process. In those early days, it was a stand-off. I would try to get out of bed. The medical staff would intercept the move and insist that I immediately get back into bed. I know they were only doing their job but I didn't see it that way. People – even if they are medical professionals – see what they want to see. And in my case, they were looking at a cripple.

In their eyes, I hadn't a clue what I was doing. But I knew exactly what I was doing. I was getting out of that bed come hell or high water.

Mr Devitt was my doctor, a consultant in orthopaedics. I had the utmost respect for him. But I was also out to defy him. Mr Devitt arrived in to see me every morning around eight, accompanied by an army of student doctors. For me it was tough trying to think clearly. I was jacked up with morphine. I was often as high as a kite. Trying to keep a grip on reality sometimes manifested itself as anger. I saw the group as a crew of eager kindergarten kids all trying to be the smartest one in the room. I fully accepted the seriousness of the students' roles but it used to annoy me that they would ignore me. It was if I was a piece of meat. There were so many times when I wanted to tell the whole lot of them to leave the room and not invade my personal space.

If I had a jaundiced view of student doctors it was because I had dated one of these students for years. I knew many of her friends very well, too well at times. They may be some of the smartest people you will ever meet but this doesn't mean that they are always the most streetwise. I thought they lived a very sheltered existence. Although they were getting ready to be surrounded by hardship every day, I often felt that they weren't prepared to deal with this hardship.

I accept that it is not fair to generalise about student doctors but my views at that time were based on my experience with students I had spent time with during college. I had had my fill of them. Now I had to put up with them ogling me every morning. I was getting fed up of their daily visits, even though I knew they were only doing their job. I wanted to run them out of the room.

One morning after they arrived for one of their sessions, I put my hand up while they were talking about me. They looked shocked. The air left the room and here was complete silence. None of them knew where to look or what to do. The chunk of meat had come alive. It had a voice.

I told them firmly that I wanted them to leave the room because I wished to speak to Mr Devitt in private. After they had traipsed out the door like scolded schoolchildren, I asked Mr Devitt if I too could leave the room. As far as I was concerned, this wasn't for the ears of the juniors. They wouldn't understand. I felt that Mr Devitt would. And he did.

Mr Devitt knew that I was getting out of bed. He could see it in my eyes. He could feel the positive energy. He rightly suggested that it might be too soon given my injuries. But he was a smart guy. He told me that if this was what I really wanted to do, he would arrange it.

Thank you, Mr Devitt.

Ten days after the accident, I was pumped up, revved up and ready for take-off. Positive mental attitude was the gas in my tank.

Iron will was the oil in my engine. I had the licence to hit the road. All I was waiting for now was the green light to press the accelerator.

That afternoon, two physiotherapists arrived into my room. Two. I didn't like this. Two suggested precaution. I didn't want to entertain those words. I wanted clear road ahead of me. I was going to do it. The two physios were obviously following the correct procedure for someone in my condition but my attitude was that procedure has no place in recovery. They approached me as if I was Humpty Dumpty – one slip and I was going to fall to pieces, smash on the ground in smithereens.

They were extremely professional, caring and considerate. They had a basic plan for me: to get out of bed and taking a few baby steps. I was not interested. This is Michael Gibbons starting the rest of his life. A few steps in the room was only a few steps inside the cage. I wanted the open plains of the corridor. If I had hair, I would have wanted to feel the breeze running through it. The corridor was the Serengeti. The tiger was uncaged.

After I got out of bed, the two physios were standing right beside me, primed to catch me if I fell. A fall at that stage could have been disastrous. It could have landed me in a wheelchair for life. I knew that. I wasn't going to be stupid but I needed to cross this mental threshold. I needed to put down a marker for the rest of my life.

After taking a few steps in the room, I made it to the door. I walked a few steps down the corridor. The girls issued a warning. They didn't want me to overdo it. They wanted me to take it easy. I took it at my pace but I kept going. Every step was a step closer to hunting down that gazelle. I made it down the long corridor. Then I turned towards the stairs. Yeah, the stairs, you read correctly. The gazelle had run up a mountain. And the tiger was taking off after it.

The girls tried to turn me away from the stairs but I wouldn't listen. To me, those stairs represented more than steps. They were a window into my future. I needed to test my mental and physical strength. I wanted to prove to myself that my consciousness, subconscious and body were all perfectly aligned, like the planets.

The physios knew I wouldn't back down. They suggested that I try a few steps. I took a few steps. And kept going. They warned me again but I refused to relent. I felt mentally strong. I decided that if I was short of physical ability, my mental strength would compensate. You can will yourself to do anything if you are in the right frame of mind.

I knew I was going to the top. Once I got to the top of the flight of stairs, I was going to go down again. And then back up again. This was the test I was setting myself. I knew that if I could meet this challenge, my path to recovery would be on a solid footing. I would be able to draw a line in the sand under my injuries, move forward and keep going.

Was it a bit reckless? Yeah. Sometimes, though, you have to be a bit reckless, go that extra mile. Over the next few days, I went up and down that stairs numerous times.

My mother said later: 'It got to the stage where it was actually a bit of a show. Doctors, nurses and patients would stand back and observe Mikey. He would have help with him but they couldn't believe the progress he was making. They were almost shocked. A couple of days earlier they thought he might never walk again. Now he was climbing stairs. They started calling him Lazarus.'

Stella, my girlfriend at the time, had arrived from New York shortly after the accident. She was a great source of assistance during these conquests of the stairs. There was plenty of fun in those journeys too. We spent a lot of time laughing when I asked her to carry my catheter as I headed off on my little expeditions.

She was delighted every time I got to the bottom of those stairs. So was everyone else. Not me. True, I had made remarkable progress. But I wanted more. It is fine to be able to achieve but to achieve consistently is the real mark of success because it proves that you are in control. So when I came down the stairs, I went back up again before it had registered with anyone. I looked at it clinically. The medication might have helped me to get up the stairs the first time but it probably wouldn't last for a second attempt. The medication was a crutch and I didn't want any assistance. So going up the stairs a second time was for me emphatic proof that I was winning the battle.

9

Races

Despite all the excellent attention and medical care patients receive, hospital becomes a depressing place after a while. It always feels stuffy and you crave fresh air in your lungs. You want to feel the breeze on your face. You want to feel alive again.

When you are involved in a serious accident, you naturally live in a bubble, the victim bubble. The victim soaks up the attention and focus. Some patients get as high on good wishes of visitors as on the drugs prescribed to cure them. It is a dangerous existence, especially when reality awaits you on the outside.

Part two of my return to reality was getting out of hospital The sooner I returned to reality, the sooner I could begin my next phase of healing. I wanted to throw off the shackles and recover as quickly as I could. I needed to take back control of my life. The first stage on that road was going home to an environment more conducive to recovery.

Of course the doctors protested. They wouldn't hear of it. But the longer I spent in hospital, the more frustrated I became. Boredom was starving my soul, draining the life out of me just as much as the pain.

I had great support in hospital. My mother and sisters were always at hand. I was never alone at any stage during the day – or even the night. My close friends Ronan and Paul often slept on the chair beside my bed. Some of the best chats I had in hospital were at four in the morning, when most of the other patients were locked down in slumber. There was a novelty to that existence. But that was all it was. And you soon become tired of novelty.

I knew there were other challenges lining up ahead of me. Apart from my physical and mental recovery, legal issues would present an equally formidable challenge. I needed a clear head to deal with these battles. And I certainly couldn't get that clarity in the haze of medication and the hospital environment that was stifling me.

I had a strong ally in my mother. She knew how determined I was. She could see the frustration seeping through my pores and she knew I had to get out. So she had a word with the doctors. She told them that she would move in with me full-time. It was enough to sway them.

Hallelujah. I was out of there.

When I got home to my house in Oranmore, I wanted my environment to be as normal as possible I didn't want to feel like a handicapped person with a carer watching over me all the time. Of course I needed help but I didn't want that help to be a crutch.

The health board wanted to revamp the house, put in a stair lift. I wouldn't have any of that. All I would agree to was a hand rail near the toilet. My mother was there and my sister, Norrie, moved in with us for a while but I always wanted my independence. I was determined to recover on my own. My house is on the flight path to Carnmore, so I constantly heard aeroplanes and helicopters on their descent. My mother used to say to me, 'How can you listen to those noises, how can they not affect you mentally?' But they never did.

Being at home allowed me my own time to grieve. I knew my life would be vastly different from before and I needed to be careful in my planning. The idea of going back to college had begun fermenting in my mind while I was in hospital and when I got home, I was convinced that this was the path I should take.

My life had changed and I needed to change with it. My

circumstances had changed. I would not be able to lift heavy boxes any longer. I certainly wouldn't be able to drive 40,000 kilometres a year, as I had done in my previous job. I needed to retrain in the medium term and needed a new career in an area in which my injuries would not restrict me.

That was for the future. For now, I needed to focus on my recovery. It was one step at a time, brick by brick in the new wall that I had to construct. It was going to be slow, tedious, testing.

I have never been a patient person. I always want to get things done and I get them done. I was aware that I would need to be patient in my recovery but I wanted to speed up the process as much as I could. I needed to test myself to see how I would cope with the new reality, push myself to see how much I could achieve.

The smart thing would have been to play it safe, maybe go for a stroll on the busy promenade in Salthill. Not me. I wanted to test myself at the Galway races. Heading to Ballybrit that race week was a big event for me, a momentous personal event, a statement that nothing was going to hold me back in this new life.

Anyone I mentioned it to thought I was completely nuts. At the time, I had a full-body cast on, like one of those corsets women used to wear in Victorian times. Every day I needed help to put it on and take it off. My family called it a cage and at times, I did feel as if I was locked inside it. I also had a cast on my arm. My big toe, would you believe, was actually one of the greatest sources of pain for me, further restricting my walk.

Going to the Galway races little more than three weeks after the accident might not be seen as the smartest of moves, especially as I decided to go on the Thursday, Ladies' Day, the busiest day of the week. I knew from personal experience that there would be close to 50,000 people there that day, many of them tipsy or drunk. A fall would be catastrophic for me but I had decided to go and no one was going to stop me. This was an immense challenge and I wanted to see how I would respond to it. Could I return to some form of reality this quickly? How would I react to crowds of people? I didn't want to dip my toes into the shallow end to test the water. I wanted to plunge straight into the deep end.

My priority was selecting the right people to go with. I knew there might be pushing and shoving but I didn't want an army of carers or bouncers around me to protect me. I knew the lads would take care of me but I also knew that they would get drunk and probably have their eyes on the women rather than on me. And who would blame them on Ladies' Day.

I came up with a plan. Two good friends, Fiona and Brenda, lived near me. I knew they would be going and that they would be getting dolled up to the nines. I also knew they would be wearing high heels. High heels are always a test. I have seen women turn into demons with the wrong shoes on. I once dated a girl in Miami who wore seven-inch heels. Yes, seven inches. If you have ever been tempted to date a girl wearing shoes like that, I'll give you one piece of advice – run. She's a witch in disguise.

I guessed how it would play out with Fiona and Brenda and the high heels. Once women have had a few drinks, the shoes get more and more uncomfortable and they start looking for a seat to take the weight off their feet. That is exactly what I needed.

I arranged for the girls to pick me up, which they graciously did. I knew this was not an ideal arrangement for them and we arrived a little later than we should have. The crowd was swollen to near capacity. Bring it on.

We walked around for a while. I was enjoying the atmosphere but I was getting a little out of breath. I didn't want to say anything because I didn't want to impose my situation on the girls and maybe ruin their day. As I had anticipated, they soon wanted to go to a quiet place to sit down and take the weight off their feet.

It was a great day. I had little interest in the horses. I didn't bet much money. I didn't drink much. But I knew I could survive in such surroundings. I knew that I could manoeuvre around my new reality. It was another step forward, another hurdle jumped, another brick in the new wall.

When the girls dropped me home, I was exhausted. Then two old friends called to the house and offered to bring me to a local pub in Oranmore. I didn't want to go. I had the perfect excuse not to go. The lads would have understood completely. But I was on a roll and I wanted to push myself. So I had a few bottles of beer in McDonagh's that evening and chatted with friends about anything and everything – but not the accident.

I was absolutely wrecked at the end of the night but really happy. It had been a tough day but I had enjoyed taking on the challenge. I knew that I was regaining control of my life. Lots of helicopters had flown in and out of the racecourse but the sight of them or the noise they made didn't have any effect on me. I was moving on.

I allowed myself a smile before I closed my eyes. Three weeks earlier, some people thought I might never walk again. Others thought I would never recover mentally, that I would be unstable, mentally fragile. Well, I never felt as strong mentally as I did that night. Once you have that mental strength, you can overcome anything.

My friends were dead but I didn't feel sad. When I thought of them I thought of the craic we would have had that day in Ballybrit if we had been there together. That's how I remembered the lads. That's how they would have wanted to be remembered.

10

School

Before the accident I always just floated through education. I was not that interested in what I was studying but I had a great ability to cram. After the accident this changed: education now became a building block in my recovery.

Most of the kids from my side of town went to a technical school but my mother wanted me to get the best education I could, in the best secondary school in Galway, Patrician College in Nun's Island, known as 'the Bish'. So, as usual – given our background – we went to see the local priest. I sat the entrance exam and was accepted. Not every student came from a well-off background but it was generally classed as a school for the privileged. Only a handful of the one hundred and fifty students enrolled at the time were from the less desirable parts of town.

We got on with our lives but sometimes our financial circumstances intruded, when a teacher or a priest came into the class looking for one of the handful of students entitled to a grant for a school uniform or schoolbooks. In fairness to our classmates, they never made an issue out of it. We were never bullied for it either. Maybe that was because of our background. It is often easier for kids to bully weaker kids from their own part of town than kids from poorer areas. A tough backgrounds usually means a tough upbringing. Kids like us were not perceived as easy targets.

I walked to school every day with my friend Jimmy. He was from the same area as me and he was also a doer. (Now he lives in a mansion overlooking Galway Bay that he built himself, he is married to Trish and they have two lovely kids.) I always felt that his real vocation was on a stage doing stand-up comedy because he is one of the funniest people you could ever meet.

Before school every morning, I would meet him on a little grassy bank near where we lived and we would head off laughing and joking. It rained very heavily one night and as I was making my way over to meet him the next morning, the entire bank moved and swallowed me up. The slope caught me and I kept sliding.

My new school uniform was ruined. My homework and books were a complete mess. When I stopped sliding, I didn't know if I was dead or alive because I couldn't see or hear a thing. Dirt was clogging my eardrums. Muck was caked all over my face, my eyes concealed behind thick layers of earth. I realised everything was OK only when I heard Jimmy and his younger brother, Jonathan, in raptures laughing at my misfortune.

I scrambled to my feet and clawed away some of the dirt from my face but I still looked like Bigfoot. I ran back to the house and showered. We were late for school but at least I looked fairly respectable. The questions started coming when my teachers checked my homework and earthworms were crawling out from beneath the pages caked with dirt.

To be honest, I hated every minute of school. I was bored and sometimes disruptive in class. With teachers, I had a reputation as a messer, while fellow students thought I was a complete gangster, someone who would try anything to get away with something. Coming up to my Junior Cert exams, I was recovering from a broken leg. Then two nights before the exams began, I woke up with intense pain in my right arm. I went to the hospital and they discovered a tumour. I was scheduled to have it removed the following day.

I was distraught. I wanted to do my exams, primarily so that

I wouldn't have to repeat the year. Another year in school would have been hell for me. (Come to think of it, it would have been hell for the teachers too.) This is my first memory of a time when I refused to let physical injury stop me doing something I wanted to do.

I got my mother and sisters to petition the Department of Education to see if they could do anything to facilitate me. The people there laughed down the phone at my sister when she outlined my plight and the plan I'd come up with. They couldn't believe that someone who had undergone a serious operation would want to begin a set of exams the following day. The fact that I couldn't write added to the absurdity of the petition.

But sheer determination got me through. I would not take no for an answer. We kept trying and my sister eventually got to speak to someone in higher authority. They came up with the idea of letting me sit the exam by speaking my answers into a tape recorder. This was unheard of at the time so you can imagine the reaction of my classmates when I arrived to sit the exams in a special room. I was already on crutches and now I had my arm in a sling. I looked like a mummy. Some of the lads thought I had tried to sabotage my body in an attempt either to avoid the exams or do them under circumstances that would guarantee me better results.

I played along with them as it was good for my reputation, something that was enhanced even further when a photograph of me appeared on the front page of the *Galway Observer*, our local free paper. I was a mini-celebrity around the school for weeks afterwards. I learned one key lesson from the whole experience: with enough determination, there is always a means of turning a disadvantage into an advantage.

Speaking into a tape recorder made little difference: my Junior Cert results were woeful. But I didn't care. When I looked back on my schooldays while studying in Columbia University twenty years later, the reason for this became very clear to me. I was bored, restless and uninterested because of the way we were taught. The teachers gave us the information and we gave it back to them in an exam. But I have always liked to make up my own mind about information. I did not realise how important education was until my changed life circumstances impelled me to retrain.

This attitude led to some clashes with teachers. The career guidance teacher told me to leave school and find work in a fast-food outlet or else get an apprenticeship as a mechanic. A mechanic? I can't even change a light bulb, never mind an exhaust pipe. Still, I could see their point. By that stage of my life, I wanted to work and earn money. When you grow up with very little, you always want more. My business skills were honed since I was very young.

I was only thirteen when one of my sisters started dating a guy whose family owned a hotel. I saw the relationship as an opportunity and begged my sister's boyfriend for a job. I pleaded with him every time I saw him until, eventually, he gave in. I got a job stacking bottles. In Irish bars, all soft drinks are supplied in glass bottles. The bottles are dumped in a skip, then sorted in plastic crates before being recycled. I worked so hard at this job that my hands would often get cut and infected. I didn't care. I was earning money and felt part of something. I loved it.

Eventually I was promoted to cleaning tables on weekend nights. By the age of sixteen, I was working behind the bar. Although I was too young to drink, I was able to sell alcohol, which sounds crazy. Working in the hotel was the best education anyone could get. I saw all sorts of crazy stuff: people having sex in the dining room, staff stealing from the kitchen, bar room brawls. Working in that hotel gave me an insight into the adult world. I watched people very closely – their mannerisms, their behaviour, how they treated others, how they reacted under the influence of alcohol, even how the hotel staff reacted under pressure. Weekend nights were powder kegs of emotions waiting to explode.

I studied sociology for three years in university but I learned more in that hotel than from any number of books I read. I was like a sponge absorbing information about human beings in action. I developed a keen awareness of people's behaviour that I retain to this day.

There was a time after my Junior Certificate when I wanted to leave school and become a hotel manager. That was until my mother sat me down one day. She told me that she would support me if I decided to do this but she imparted one crucial piece of advice – I would be working when everyone else was off and I would be off when everyone else was either working or in school. I remember thinking, 'No way, I want to be off when the girls are off.'

So I put the head down and worked hard. In the mock exams before the Leaving Certificate, I did really well. On the day we got our mock results, one of my teachers said he could not believe I had got a B. I was smiling down at the back of the class and he took issue with me. He said I hadn't done a stroke of work and that there was no way I could have achieved those results by fair means.

I was absolutely livid. I was never afraid to fight my corner so I marched straight down to the principal's office and demanded that the teacher apologise to me. That was not something you did in that school in the early 1990s but I didn't care. When I got no joy, I went home and told my mother.

She did not take it well. The next morning, she was on the phone and arranged to come into school. She spoke to the principal and told him that she wasn't prepared to let this lie. The principal asked me what I needed and I told him I expected an apology from the teacher in front of the whole class. He had accused me in front of everyone else. Now I wanted him to apologise in front of the same people.

When I look back on it I am amazed at the cheek I had. But the principal agreed and the teacher said he was sorry. When he asked me if I accepted his apology, I said I did. We became great friends later on in life and I think he always respected me for standing up to him. I got a surge of power from the stance I had taken. It helped me feel in control, which was something I had always craved. My mother and two sisters had been a massive influence in forming me as a person but I always felt I needed to assert myself in the male environment of school.

When I was sixteen I was elected a class prefect. We had to clear out the classrooms and man the doors at lunch break and I took pride in my job. I made a good prefect. I also loved the power that came with it.

In our final year, an election was held for head prefect. The contest was between Mike, Derek and me. Mike plagued the teacher in charge of the selection process but my past eventually caught up with me. Some teachers voted against me and I was named vice-prefect instead. Derek was named head prefect. This episode left me with the salutary lesson: always close the door gently or it could swing back and take your fingers off.

Even though we had been rivals Mike and I cooperated well. At the time, the school ran the 'Bish' discos, supervised by the principal, Brother Marcus. It was a very Catholic Ireland way of introducing boys and girls and making some money in the process. Brother Marcus used to call Mike and me into the office the school morning after the disco and pay us £20 for our help in running the event. We pulled in more people and made more money so we felt entitled to a far greater recompense than £20.

Mike approached me one day about running discos on our own. I knew we could do it. It was a win-win situation. We could make money, meet girls and be the men about town. So we set up Steinberg promotions, and actually *were* the men about town for our age. The marketing was mostly left up to me while Mike had a great way with people, which he later proved by becoming a city councillor and mayor of Galway.

Our plan was simple. We approached one girls' secondary school and pitched the idea of an exclusive disco between our schools. Not only would this annoy the other Galway schools where our fellow classmates had girlfriends – it created a huge buzz around the event.

A week before the disco, when demand from the girls' school was at its highest, we dumped as many tickets as we could on the market. Girls from other schools started hoovering them up. We also insisted that the guys in our school buy an extra ticket. This ensured that there were more than enough girls to go around. I reckon the girl-boy ratio was at least 3:1. Bingo.

Our boys had a field day. It was like shooting fish in a barrel. The girls were throwing themselves at the lads. We were heroes. I only ever got one complaint from a guy in school and I told him that I had filled a hall with three hundred women and that it was his fault, not mine, if he couldn't land one of them.

Mike and I kept the discos going for a while and they were a massive success. He met his future wife at one of them and I met a girl I dated for many years. We made a bag of cash from the venture. I can remember us each making £300 profit from one disco. In the early 1990s, this was serious, serious cash for eighteen-year-olds. It was no wonder that we were able to go out every Friday and Saturday night for months afterwards.

The discos also gave me my first brush with jealousy. Many people criticised us for making so much money out of our own classmates and other students but they did not take into account the effort we put into making those nights such a success. It was a huge drain on our time and we were always gambling that the attraction would hold. If it wore off and no one turned up, we were the ones who were going to be out of pocket.

It was also during one of those events that I was first double-crossed over money. We had hired a tough guy from school as the chief bouncer. He was good at his job but it went to his head.

He thought he was Vin Diesel or Vinnie Jones so he decided to ramp up the stakes. He invited a number of guys to cause trouble. I knew there might be a riot if I let them in because they were only there to fight. That would have been catastrophic for the school and it could have finished our venture so I stood at the door and refused them entry. The bouncer protested their innocence but I wasn't for turning and he went back to his job.

At the end of the night, after the place had cleared out, Mike and I counted the money, paid whoever had to be paid and split the profits. But before we left we heard that our friends were waiting outside, threatening to unleash all sorts of hell on us. I will admit that I was nervous but I had a few big guys with me and we said we would take our chances. As soon as we came out the back door, the gang jumped us. Fists were flying and a huge scrap started. But clearly they hadn't done their homework. Mike and I were carrying a small fortune and we should have been the primary targets. As they were more intent on unloading punches than uploading their pockets, Mike ran right and I sprinted left. We knew that the other big lads could take care of themselves, plus they had been paid for the services they provided earlier in the night.

I might not have been as talented academically as most of the students in my class in college but I had a lot of business experience under my belt. I learned as much from organising those school discos as I would have done from studying a multitude of books on marketing and economics. The foundation of most of the course work in organisational psychology that I completed in Columbia had been solidly laid fifteen years earlier around the streets of Galway.

I also had a respectable third-level education behind me when I went to Columbia. Despite all my messing in school, I earned enough points in my Leaving Certificate to get into NUI Galway. I took ar Arts degree in history, politics and sociology. I got by. I didn't kill myself studying but I got an honours degree. Immediately after graduating, I did a post-grad in health promotion. After I left college, I worked for several different companies as a medical representative.

I did well in that area but I have always pursued business interests in my spare time. I am a kind of insomniac and have been able to get by with three or four hours of sleep a night. Part of the reason is that I find it hard to switch my brain off. I am always thinking up ideas for making money. I didn't need to study business to hone these skills.

For success you need courage and neck, qualities I never lacked. There is one standout memory from my time in NUIG. In third year, our final year, we were doing a sociology course, 'Data Based Stats'. I hadn't a clue. I hadn't any interest in the area either. The course was in second semester, between Christmas and summer. In March, the lecturer came in one day with a wonderful idea. He planned to pre-release the exam paper. He intended to hand out an exam paper with twelve questions. On the day, four of those questions would appear and we would have to complete three.

In one way, it made perfect sense. Students would have to cover all the areas of the course to ensure that they weren't caught out on the day. Plus, from the student's perspective, it was a very fair system; if you put in the work, studied and researched all the questions, you would be guaranteed a good result.

To some of us, though, this was a vision of hell. It meant that we couldn't circumvent the system by leaving out certain areas of the course. In other words, the gamblers had very little to bet on.

The lecturer wanted to be fair to everyone, not impose the paper on the class without putting it to a vote. Before the vote was taken, I turned into a blitz politician, canvassing everyone around me and within earshot for a no vote. But apart from a few of my buddies I may as well have been speaking to the wall. The vote was carried by about 85 per cent.

As far as I was concerned, this was unacceptable. We had to do something. My friend Christy and I marched upstairs to the lecturer's office about ten minutes after the lecture had finished. He didn't know us from Adam but we invited ourselves in. We basically told him that he was off his head to pre-release an exam paper and suggested that he reconsider his decision.

When I think back on it now, we were off our heads. It was enough to get us kicked out of the university although, in fairness to the lecturer, he didn't dismiss us out of hand but engaged with our concerns. But he must have been laughing at our neck.

After our failed attempt, for the next few weeks we were like dealers on the black market. We spent more time bartering and swapping questions than anything else. If we had spent the same amount of time studying the questions, we would have got straight As. In the end, I got a C.

It is important to work hard. But it is as important to have fun in the process. I remind people of this every day of my life. You have to live life to the maximum, enjoy every minute because you could fall out of the sky tomorrow and the show will be over.

11

Legal

My mother has a saying and I have never heard her say a truer word: 'There is justice. And then there is the law.'

Anyone who has faced the legal system in Ireland will probably acknowledge this. I don't think it is the fault of the judges. They have one of the most difficult jobs in the country, firstly because of our huge compensation culture and secondly because the system fosters that culture.

My observations are those of a layman, so many people in the profession may disagree. But come and sit on the other side of the table before you disagree.

In Irish law the survivor of an accident sues the person responsible for their injuries. If that person is insured, the insurance company pays out. I am not saying that Damien was responsible for the accident but this is how the system works. For a start, this was very difficult for me. It was deeply upsetting that I had to sue Damien personally and, in effect, his elderly parents, for whom I had such respect and affection. This couple had enough legal problems to take care of – I was another one popping up in front of them.

I was also acutely aware how this would look to other people. I was suing my best friend, who had saved my life. Think of the optics of that scenario for a second. It would be natural for people to perceive me as a bloodsucking beast, draining the life out of the family of my dead friend. I have never worried about what people think but dealing with innuendo and speculation and gossip was difficult for me as Damien's name was inextricably involved the whole time.

I have always tried as hard as I could to respect my friend's memory and do the right thing but I also had to think of myself and keep an eye on the bigger picture. Would I ever be able to work again? How was I going to provide for myself in the long term? How was I going to live?

We all have to do some things in life that we don't really want to do and I needed to face the reality of what was ahead of me. So I arranged to meet Damien's brother, Brendan, like Damien a gentleman. I told Brendan I was deeply unhappy about having to go down this route and I asked him what he really thought. I wanted to establish what the family's feelings were because the last thing I wanted to do was heap more hurt on their already unbearable pain.

Brendan said that while it was in Damien's name I was suing, I was, in effect, suing his estate and the estate was fully insured. This gave me great peace of mind. I was put even more at ease when I discussed the issue with Damien's parents. It felt as if someone had lifted a massive weight off my shoulders. I needed this clarity because it did not take me long to realise the enormousness of the challenge I was facing. I was taking on a huge insurance company. In their eyes, I was a statistic, not a human being who had been seriously injured. They did not care about me. All they cared about was paying me the least amount they could get away with.

It was a tricky task and I didn't want to lose my soul or my dignity in the process. However, I made a deliberate decision to pursue this long, tortuous process. From the beginning, my aim was to get enough compensation to secure my future and take care of my family. In times of crisis, you have to set clear goals. At this stage, I was working my way through these goals: getting out of bed, trying to live a normal life; ensuring my financial future. My long-term goals included returning to college but that couldn't happen until I'd achieved my medium-term goals.

By the time I got out of hospital and began living my life again, the reality of that new life soon dawned on me. I was effectively imprisoned in my own home. Unable to drive, I had to hire a part-time driver. Before long, I settled on a very basic and straightforward routine, day after day, week after week, extending into year after year.

Every morning, a taxi would pick me up at eleven and either drive me to town or to my mother's house. I came home again at 2pm and at 6.30pm I went to the sauna for an hour to try to loosen out my aching muscles. I was back home by 7.30pm and there I stayed until eleven the following morning, when the routine would begin all over again. I used to find Saturday and Sunday particularly harrowing. I might go out for a few hours on a Saturday night but when I got home, it would be almost thirty-six hours before I got out again.

I understand that some people face far worse ordeals and traumas. Some people can't walk and will never walk again. Others are blind. Still others are bedridden. I appreciated what I had. But trying to deal with the change, especially when I was a complete night owl, was a massive challenge. It was a constant battle not to let negativity consume me, not to surrender my life to the accident. I had longer-term plans but all I could do at that moment was get stronger and recover.

I had to turn negatives into positives. One advantage of having so much time on my hands was that it gave me the opportunity to reflect on the accident. I took notes. I read up on legal issues related to similar accidents, preparing for the legal minefield I was about to enter.

Shortly before the accident, I had already had some experience of the legal system in Ireland. I had invested in a business, rather naïvely, as it turned out. Things went pear-shaped between me and the majority owners. Matters escalated and after various attempts to sort things out we were headed for court. It was a risky road for me to pursue given that all my money was tied up in this venture but Mark had secured a loan for me, while Damien was funding the court case. It wasn't a nice experience but I was determined to see it through.

Then the accident happened and everything changed.

For a start, I wasn't able to go to law with my partners. At that stage, it wasn't worth my time or my energy. I needed my strength to fight other battles, starting with my recovery.

While I was in hospital, my mother told me that I needed to get out of the business and sort out the financial side of things. This was absolutely crucial because I had no idea what type of recovery I would make. I was still in a terrible state physically, my body wrecked by injury and trauma. To really rub salt into a heap of open wounds, I had contracted the hospital bug, MRSA. But the whole affair ended up in court after all. I eventually achieved what I wanted but it took an awful lot out of me.

What the whole affair taught me is that when you get involved in a legal case, everything goes askew and commonsense often disappears out the window. The law is concerned only with the law, not with any individual. What might seem wrong to someone in moral or human terms can appear to be OK in the guise of a legal process. There is no humanity in that process.

The experience left a deep impression on me. I remember making a mental note to myself that this was only the start of it, that I would have to be ultra-committed to see my injury case through. I was also fully aware that I was in this by myself, with no one to help me. I had no friends. The legal fallout was bound to be horrendous and I would have to face the entire challenge head-on.

In the aftermath of a serious accident, it soon becomes apparent that the injured person's relationships with the legal and medical professions are intertwined. It certainly didn't take me long to realise how much I was at the mercy of the whims of these professionals.

Medical professionals are ultra-professional, yet acutely aware of the pending legal cases of the people they treat, so they record everything. On the other hand, my solicitor's job was to interpret the medical data and mould my case accordingly. Before long, you realise that you really are only a number or a case to these people, nothing more.

Once I fully grasped this, clarity came to me again. I knew that there would be lots of players at the table and that I needed to take control of the situation quickly. If I did not, things could slip out of my control and, if that happened, it was possible that I would lose my say in the whole process. In situations like this, too many people are willing to accept the role of victim, happy for others to take over the running. When they finally seek to have a voice in the process, it is drowned out or is no longer relevant, especially when they go into court. You can go in there and scream at the top of your voice but unless you clearly identify your case and what you want no one will hear you.

This was totally alien to me but I needed to get up to speed on all the pending legal cases. I needed to be clear and single-minded, to have cold-blooded conviction, because the suits on the other side of the courtroom would have the mindset of a bunch of assassins. I also accepted what this was likely to entail. Years of court cases. *Years.* Not easy to get your head around.

The biggest advantage I had was time. The second was the experience I had of my previous court case and the clarity I had gained from it. If you are involved with the law, law must come first. I am not saying I was happy with this attitude but it was clearly one I had to develop if I were to survive in the legal jungle, particularly with the level of compensation I was looking for.

Given my injuries, I was going to fight for as much compensation as I felt I deserved. I was lucky that I had a strong mind but

I didn't have a healthy body. My attitude made up for the deficit. I made up my mind that I was in charge here, not any legal person. I had a great team around me, particularly my lead solicitor, but I never lost sight of the fact that I was one of a number of cases for these people. They went home every day and probably didn't give a second thought to my physical or mental wellbeing. Could you blame them? They had their own lives to live and they spent time pondering my health only when they had space in their diaries to do so.

My legal team consisted of two senior barristers, one junior, two solicitors and an accountant. Individually, they were nice people but when they were put together in a room, they would attempt to influence me, always moving things towards their goals, not mine.

The bottom line was that they always wanted to settle. More than 90 per cent of cases in Ireland are settled, mostly on the steps of the court. For me another major revelation was that once the brief is filed, with each side's claims and counter claims, the legal team gets more than 80 per cent of the fees. Going to court is not financially appealing to them because they have already secured most of their fees and are paid only a small fee for a day in court.

The main body of work is assembled long before you get near the courtroom. You have to have numerous medical examinations before the legal teams interpret what the doctors have said. I learned very early on that one line in a medical report could be interpreted very differently by the opposing legal teams, rendering all my other medicals obsolete. That is why it was so important to keep the case study coherent and always to the point. In the end, a judge would have to hear oral evidence from me on the entire case.

You could easily be confused and feel almost concussed by the relentless medical and legal reports but I knew I had one massive advantage in dealing with the barrage of information. My first job after leaving college was as a pharmaceutical sales representative. Then I moved into hospital sales before becoming a product specialist. So I had had a lot of experience of dealing on a daily basis with medical consultants, even some professors.

My job was simple. Without being pushy, forceful or false, I would use a detailed aid to get across three to five points about the merits of my drug as opposed to others. Companies spent fortunes training us. We would spend days at conferences simply reciting the detailed aid in simulated exercises in front of colleagues. The exercises were taped and repeatedly studied to fine-tune our approach.

The best training was when actors were brought in to play the role of doctors. They pushed us hard in very realistic role play. It was a great learning experience – and how thankful I was for it once I came to my own legal proceedings. This training was invaluable when it came to my court case. I had the skillset to get my point across to the doctors, focusing on my goal but at all times keeping my case study coherent.

No matter where I turned, I was able to borrow from the skills bank in which I had deposited so much during my twenties During that time, I had visited general practitioners all over the country and dealt with consultants in a broad range of medical disciplines. I had travelled to Europe for meetings in the company of medical professionals. In short, I had spent plenty of time in their company.

From all that time socialising with them, I had a unique lay person's take on the medical profession. Doctors are not gods. They are highly trained professionals. They are no smarter than the average person. What sets them apart is that they have extensive training in something that is very important to us all – our health. This can make them appear godlike in their work because people put their trust in them to make them feel better.

I never had an inflated perception of the medical profession. I dealt with them long enough to see that they have the same anxieties and faults as everyone else. But my insight into how they thought and acted gave me a real edge in my legal case because I knew how to get my opinion across to them without any fear of contradiction or skewed interpretation. After a while, I could read the pattern of the long-drawn-out compensation process like a book. One doctor would give a prognosis on my injuries. Then the insurance company would disagree and give an almost comp-letely different assessment. How can two trained professionals in a field as precise as medicine come to such a vastly different conclusions? It was almost like modern art: one viewer looks at an abstract painting and sees a man playing a violin; another sees, in the same painting, the same man about to unleash hell with a baseball bat.

I remember asking one doctor if he was biased. Trust me, this man was never asked that question before in his life. He was incredulous and responded by asking why I would think that was possible. I gave it to him straight – that I had genuine concerns that he was working for the insurance company and was biased in their favour. The guy nearly fell off the chair. In the end, he gave a fair and balanced report and was not called upon to testify. Draw your own conclusions as to why.

I was not prepared to let anything go. I often asked doctors, before I left their rooms, what they were going to write in their reports. I felt that I had every right to know. This often didn't go down well, as if I had some cheek even to question their authority and credibility. But why wasn't I entitled to this information about my health when a large fee was changing hands?

When an insurance company is involved you are fair game, a legitimate target. Of course I understand why. People are abusing the system left, right and centre every day of the week. This is the reason your insurance premiums go through the roof. Often, there is no honour on either side. Insurance companies don't want to part with their money, even when a person is genuinely injured and within their rights to sue. The victim often has an inflated expectation of the award and feels that they will never fully recover.

That is why you have to be absolutely unwavering in your beliefs when you go into court. The other side will always try to scare you, get you running for cover. They will prey on any weakness or insecurities you have. And if they think you're stumbling, they'll try to bury you. They will come at you from every angle.

Judges have a very difficult job trying to arrive at the truth because the culture is very underhand in these situations. When I arrived at one of the mediation sessions, I was told that the reason I was putting off the court case was because I was getting married. It was news to me. I had broken up with the girl in question about eighteen months beforehand.

I always knew I was good with the ladies. But not so good that a girl I hadn't been with for almost two years would want to walk me up the aisle.

You couldn't make it up.

12

Circles

For four full years, my life was one endless circle of law. You start at one point and keep coming back to it. I often felt as if I was carrying the weight of the world on my shoulders. The legal world feels so heavy because it drains the energy and life out of you and intravenously pumps negativity into your bloodstream.

No matter where you turn, you can't get away from it. A barrage of phone calls. Solicitor's letters. Meetings. Consultations. Briefings. For four years, it was everywhere. Every turn, thought, action and reaction involved some elements of consideration of the pending court case.

You want to scream. The only reason you don't is because this is what you have signed up for. Once you go to court, you have to accept what the whole process entails. It becomes harder to accept as the years pass and the process drags on. But the end will come some day – and, you hope, with the outcome you desire – and this is what keeps you going.

Would I become rich as a result of this case? Not a chance. Was I motivated by money? Absolutely not. I was being practical. Not cynical or immoral: practical. All I was doing was trying to secure my future.

The High Court in Dublin is one of the strangest places you could imagine. If you were writing a novel, it would be a great place to get information and inspiration: material drips off the walls there. It is like a human mart. The ordinary people are the cattle and the barristers and solicitors are the farmers trying to trade a good deal. Barristers are merely a product of their environment. Horse traders. Trust me, if you don't have a reasonably honest barrister, he will sell you out. Why? Because you are probably one of a multitude of cases on his or her desk. In theory, all cases are individual. Yet in reality, when opposing barristers meet, they discuss cases they are both handling and 'doing favours' is commonplace. I have lived this and I know what goes on.

You automatically assume that barristers and solicitors are some of the most intelligent, honest and upright people you could ever meet, as well as being competent and focused. My experience was that some of them are and some of them are – well– not.

During my two weeks in the High Court, I was sitting in the canteen one day with some of my team. We were discussing a critical part of the case. We were all listening very intently to what one of the team had to say when he suddenly blurted out, 'I love Chinese girls.'

I, along with everyone else in his company, followed his line of vision. An Asian trainee barrister had walked by. This guy had the rest of my life in his hands and all he could think about was a woman! Although I suppose you could argue that he was adding some light to a dark and heavy process.

As we came closer to the hearing, I decided to get a new lead senior counsel. As far as I was concerned, there was too much talk about settlement. I needed my team to be certain of one thing – I was going through with this. I also knew my team would relay that conviction to the other side so the insurance company would also be made aware of my determination to see this out to the bitter end. We were going to court.

No one wanted to go down that road. I didn't. But I needed my legal team to think that I was obsessive in my determination to have my day on the stand, like some veteran warrior who wants to unload all his battle stories. To achieve my goal, I felt that I needed to inject some new blood into my team. Complacency is another by-product of prolonged court cases so I needed to create some healthy competition between the legals. When I regenerated my legal team after four years on the road, everyone on board was driven and prepared for court.

This move provided me with a lot of interesting insights into how legal people work. In case conferences, I would challenge the new lead council and watch the others smile when I caught him out. I knew the workings of the case inside out. I had spent weeks, months, even years, poring over every detail, whereas the new man had more than likely read over the papers ten minutes before coming into the meeting.

Again, my pharmaceutical training was invaluable. During the time I worked in sales, I would have case conferences, study days and small meetings, in which I was repeatedly challenged about the merits of my products and the messages I was given to sell them. I was grilled by forceful, intelligent people, like my legal team. The pharmaceutical industry invested a small fortune in that type of training and I made maximum benefit of it when I was preparing my case.

My barristers kept saying that medical reports had to be greater than 50 per cent to dispel any reasonable doubt. In other words, a judge looks at medical reports, psychological analyses, victim testimony and so on to assess whether that evidence is more or less than 50 per cent in the victim's favour. It was always my intention to prove to the judge that my case was far above 50 per cent.

I tried to manage the situation as well as possible but I could never once drop my guard or think I was in full control. This gave me the edge I needed. Given that the case was effectively an assessment of damages only and how much money I would receive, I knew from the very beginning that private investigators would be all over me.

I had two private investigators on my heels at all times. One was a local guy who would follow me around when I was in Galway. When I was in Dublin, a team of specialists would track my every move, especially on nights out. It was a pretty horrible experience. It wasn't as if I was suddenly going to start doing cartwheels down a street after a skin load of drink, or start dancing on tables, but it still took a huge mental toll. You could never switch off, never fully relax. It often felt like being imprisoned in a mobile cell: wherever you went, whatever you did, you had bars around you, preventing you from living a full life.

I remember being in a nightclub one time close to the court date and seeing a blonde girl. She was standing beside me and a group of friends but had her back turned to us. For some reason – I was particularly sensitive because of the court date being so close – I got it into my head that she was a private investigator. Of course she wasn't a PI but this was the sort of fear and anxiety that the case inflicted on me. I had put everything into the case from the point of view of research and preparation but the case colonised my mind in many other ways. It ruled, owned my life.

One night, I was in Busker Browne's pub in Galway city with my cousin and her friends. They decided to go to Halo nightclub and I said I'd go along. At one point, my cousin asked me to go out dancing. I told her I never dance. 'I'm the worst dancer in the world,' I said. She tried to persuade me but I wasn't having it.

A couple of weeks later, the barristers from the two sides met and one of them said to a member of my legal team: 'We have a video of your client dancing in Halo nightclub.'

When they told me, I was emphatic. 'No they don't.'

'Yes they do,' he replied.

'Tell them to show me so,' I responded.

'They won't show it now. They will only show it in court.'

I had absolutely no doubts in my mind. 'Go back to that guy and tell him straight out that there is no video.'

They refused to show me the video. It was then (correctly) explained to me that in a courtroom, an audio/video presentation could be a disaster for me. No matter how you argued against it, a judge could take a different view if you are standing on the edge of a dance floor when you are supposed to be almost half crippled. Watching a video in a courtroom at 10am, a judge could very easily decide that you are putting on a big act and award accordingly.

When you go to court, you have to have 100 per cent conviction. You can't lie or bluff. The barristers on the other side of the fence will smell it a mile off and will cut you down like a tree. But I knew I had nothing to fear. I looked my barrister in the eye and said to him, 'I will go into court because that video doesn't exist. I don't dance. You won't see me dancing in a nightclub.'

It was a key test but I needed to be strong. My own legal team didn't believe me. I didn't care. I was trying to manage this situation as best I could. 'I'm telling you, there's no video. If they say there's a video, let's go to court and face it head on.'

We were put on the list. We got a date. We were going to court. Our diaries were cleared. The circle of law, the never-ending circle, seemed to get even wider. More negotiations. More dialogue. Horse-trading at its purest. All the while, I had the courage of my convictions.

Eventually, the other side came back and said that the video was not as clear as they thought it was. No shit. I don't dance and a girl I was once going out with broke up with me because of this.

But we were still going to court. So we waited and waited to be called. And all the while, I had private investigators discreetly following me around as if I was some rock star, as if they were paparazzi trying to get the one big-money shot. I rang my solicitor and he told me there was nothing they could do about it. The only consolation in the whole messy ordeal was that the endgame was in sight.

Finally, the end of my legal case came more quickly than I expected. It took less than fifteen minutes. I refused the first offer because I have a rule in life never to accept the first offer. It is not my style. So the case opened. Day one began. I was due to give evidence on day two.

Another offer, a reasonable figure. I was happy. I accepted it.

Thanks be to God.

It was 11 July 2009, almost four years to the day since the crash happened. I felt I had finally got my life back.

The following day, this report appeared in *The Irish Times*:

The sole survivor of a helicopter crash, in which the pilot and another man died, has secured more than €1 million in settlement of his High Court action.

Michael Gibbons (34), Oranmore, County Galway, who sustained head and other injuries in the crash, continues to have frequent nightmares and suffers post-traumatic stress disorder as a result, the court heard. Doctors had described him as remaining significantly incapacitated and feeling depressed and guilty over surviving the accident.

Mr Gibbons was the only survivor of the crash on 9 July, 2005, near Derrybrien, County Galway, involving a Robinson R44 helicopter piloted by Damien Bergin, which was returning from the Tall Ships race in Waterford.

Mr Bergin (32), Castleblakeny, Co Galway, and Mark Reilly (49), Clybaun Road, Galway, died of multiple injuries when the helicopter crashed into a wooded area in the Slieve Aughty mountains.

Mr Gibbons, Clochog, Oranmore, County Galway, had sued the representatives of the estate of Mr Bergin and two companies, Donville Helis Ltd, Derrydonnell, Oranmore, and 21st Century Aviation Ltd, Deerpark Industrial Estate, Oranmore, respectively the owner and hirer/operator of the helicopter.

Mr Gibbons alleged negligence, breach of duty and breach of

contract against all defendants. On the second day of the hearing
yesterday, Mr Justice John Quirke was told the case had been settled
and could be struck out.

No details were disclosed, but the settlement is understood to be in
excess of €1 million.

Aside from my case, there were other legal ramifications, issues for
Mark's and Damien's families, that had to be ironed out in court.
Friends said to me that I had to put all that to one side, that it was
inevitable collateral damage of taking the case. I fully accepted this
from when I first took the case but it didn't make it any easier to
deal with.

Mark had got divorced not long before the accident and his
solicitor had suggested making a will but Mark never did. Dying
is usually the last thing on your mind. But his dying without a
will triggered legal issues in relation to properties he co-owned,
some of which were among the most valuable in Galway. That was
Galway in the boom times.

I never got involved in the cases involving the estates. It was
none of my business. By that stage, I was absolutely scalded from
legal proceedings and court cases. For me, all that was firmly
in the past. I was moving forward, finally ready to start living
again. I had desperately wanted my life back and now I had it.
Because of the litigation process that dragged on for four years, it
was very difficult to make a full recovery from my injuries. This
was as much mental as physical because the two were so closely
intertwined during the case. There were frequent reminders of
the accident. Mark and Damien were constantly being spoken
about in terms of what happened that day. There were forests of
medical and actuarial reports. There were times when I couldn't
look over my shoulder without wondering if a private investigator
was behind me. That in itself produces a degree of paranoia, which
in turn breeds constant and draining negativity.

I had were some very low days during those four years but I always had the belief that I would eventually get the award I felt I deserved. I wanted to do it and I did it.

I now had a degree of security. I know money alone doesn't bring happiness. It certainly won't reduce the pain in your body or laser your mental scars. But it armed me to construct the next phase of my life. I was determined to build a good one.

I will never forget the day the case finally ended. I can still clearly see the usher coming into the room for the last time. I had a quick consultation with my legal team. They asked me if I wanted to go back into court to hear the judge delivering the settlement summary but I had no interest in doing so. I had been listening to legal jargon for four years. I couldn't take in another word.

I walked out of the Four Courts that day into the bright sunshine and loosened my tie. For the first time in four years, I finally felt I could breathe.

13

PTSD

If Paradise is what they say it is, I was there at Christmas 2002. It was Maya Beach in Ko Phi Phi Leh Island, off the coast of Thailand, where the movie *The Beach* was filmed. A group of us, including Damien, had gone there for Christmas and when the rest of the party went home, I stayed an extra week there with my friend Derek. We dropped out of life for a few weeks and landed in Paradise. It was so good, you never wanted to leave.

On New Year's Eve 2002, we partied the night away on the stump of a tree at a local bar, more like a run-down beach hut. This was living at its purest. We didn't need drink because we were intoxicated on life. I had never been so happy. After ringing in the New Year, we returned to our beach huts. Before long, we heard singing and the sound of a drum. We decided to investigate, as we wanted more and didn't want the night to end. We listened to the music and met new friends. We shared an unforgettable experience, as we waited on the beach until the sun came up to herald a new year and a new beginning. I remember thinking that this was going to be one of the greatest years of our lives.

During my recovery, I often thought about that time. A year later, almost to the day, Ko Phi Phi Leh Island was swept up in a giant wave. The tsunami that resulted from a massive earthquake hundreds of miles away tore this paradise apart. A year earlier, I was one of the holidaymakers who had basked in the most glorious tranquillity imaginable. Now all the people who were on the island had their lives ripped apart. One minute they were in paradise. The next minute, through no fault of their own, they were in a living hell.

One image from that disaster resonated with me, an image I have seen many times on television. A lone person was lying at the water's edge with not a care in the world. The next minute the waters started to retreat. Little did that man realise that his own ocean of life was also retreating. The end was only seconds away.

As the horror slowly dawned on him, that man seemed frozen in shock. He decided to sit and wait for the inevitable. Maybe he was paralysed by fear and couldn't move. I have thought many times about what was going through his head. Perhaps he thought it was a dream and that this hell could surely not be visiting him in paradise, that if he sat there and waited he would snap out of the nightmare. But there was no suspending this reality. The man was wiped out in an instant.

Throughout my recovery, this image became a recurring theme. On the day of the crash, I too was on Ko Phi Phi Island, living the dream with my best friends. Of course I was like everyone else in that I had the stresses of life to deal with but I was wading in the ocean of existence. Moments later, we entered the fog and the ocean of my life retreated. As we crashed through the trees we were like the lone person on the water's edge. This could not be happening. But the forest kept coming, like the ocean, until, eventually, we were swallowed up by the giant wave of trees.

I got lucky, unlike Mark and Damien. Thankfully, my life experiences up to that point had provided me with something to cling on to. I was safe. I would recover. I was determined that I would. But on the road to recovery, the monkey that is PTSD jumped firmly on to my back.

I am fortunate to have a very tight family unit. I am blessed that I had the two best counsellors you could ever ask for – my mother and my sister Karen. Any time I was upset or feeling down, I knew

I could talk to them. When I felt the walls closing in around me, they were the ones who pushed them back away from me. We will always find our own path in life, or else someone will be sent along to direct us on that path, even if they often appear to be the most unlikely guides imaginable. I repeat these words to myself so often that I can sing them like a nursery rhyme.

One incident soon after the accident proved this. The legal circus had begun by now and my goal was simple: I wanted to get a fair damages award so that money would never be too big a concern for me again as I went about rebuilding my life. To this day, I still can't sit anywhere for a long period of time. Working in a normal environment is not physically possible. Driving is not really an option. So I needed security.

I had established a routine to speed my recovery because routine provides stability. Because of the extent of my injuries, I found it very hard to sleep. I could only manage a few hours at night. I would get up at 10am before returning to bed at 2pm to try to snaffle a few more hours' rest.

On one particular morning, a nurse was due to visit at 10. I waited and waited and waited. When there was no sign of her by 2pm, I followed my usual routine and went back to bed for a few hours. What was I supposed to do? I hadn't received a phone call to tell me she wasn't coming.

Not long after my head hit the pillow, she arrived. The waiting must have drained the life out of me because, on that particular day, I almost collapsed into a coma with tiredness. My mother – who was always by my side during that time – tried to wake me but she couldn't.

As a result of that incident, the nurse made a diagnosis that I was seriously depressed and needed immediate help.

She went to my orthopaedic surgeon, along with the physician I was seeing at that time, and claimed that I was slipping into a black hole, an abyss of depression that could do irretrievable damage to my mental health. I thought the whole thing was a joke. If she had come on time, or had the courtesy to let me know she would be four hours late, she would not have come up with that diagnosis.

As soon as she snapped her fingers, I was in front of a doctor. I didn't know about the nurse's diagnosis but as soon as I arrived into the room, I knew something was up. There was another nurse there along with the doctor, which I found unusual. The first question the doctor asked was how I was 'feeling mentally.' Was I having nightmares? He explained the background to the questions, which was framed by the nurse's concerns. They had decided to send me to a psychologist but the next available appointment wasn't for three weeks.

A light bulb went off in my head. I didn't feel depressed. My mental health was fine. But since I had a major legal case coming up, all this stuff was suddenly very interesting. If this was the medics' reaction because I had taken a nap in the afternoon, what must they really be thinking about my mental state after I had survived a helicopter crash that killed my two best friends? They must be thinking my brain was a mass of sludge, that I was a total basket case – and if those doctors thought like this about my mental health, what might a judge think?

I was not trying to defraud the system. I had been seriously injured, through no fault of my own. My life had been turned upside down. I had no idea what lay ahead of me and all I was doing was looking for was a fair settlement. But because it was an insurance claim, I knew the insurance company would do their utmost to deny me as much of that settlement as they possibly could.

So I needed to be armed for this process and the conversation with the doctor was a huge moment in determining the outcome. Yes, I had suffered from depression. Yes, I had some terrible flash-backs. Yes, I had some awful nightmares. Yes, I had survivor guilt.

But I never felt that any of those realities were attacking my overall mental health. I still felt in control. Guilt and depression weren't dictating my life.

Of course I had good days and bad days. This is inevitable, especially when you are imprisoned in your own house for so much of the time. Your mental health can go from high to low in the course of a day. But when you know you are facing a legal case that could drag on for years, you cannot lose your focus, although it would be easy to give in to the fears and anxieties associated with it.

After the accident, everyone had talked so much about PTSD that I expected it to hit me like a sledgehammer as the months passed. Surely it would come at me some day like a stealth bomber and begin dropping warheads on my consciousness. Although there were strains of PTSD running through my life they weren't running my life. But I knew that my case, which would be adjudicated by an impartial judge, would be based primarily on whether or not I suffered from PTSD. So I needed to make it very clear in my case study.

How do you explain PTSD? A lot of the symptoms doctors and nurses had spoken about came to pass and I did have some very bad days – but for me the symptoms were not as they are portrayed in textbooks. And certainly not as they are portrayed in the media. I have met people whose lives have been ruined by PTSD and I do not doubt for a second the impact it can have. But I never felt it in those terms. Again, my survival personality had kicked in.

So how did I cope? How did I win my battle with PTSD?

Initially, I was fine mentally. This was no surprise as PTSD does not kick in immediately. The longer I waited for it to hit me, the stronger I became, the more prepared I was for the fight.

My mind was already battling with my body, refusing to let my injuries take control of my life. I was finding a place to store the pain in my subconscious. What had happened had happened so I needed to accept the facts as they were.

That was a key theme for my PTSD. I accepted it for what it was. PTSD occurs when your body and mind are not in tune. When you sleep, your subconscious keeps reacting to the trauma because your mind is not on the same wavelength as your body. So I did my best to keep them on the same frequency. By maintaining a routine and planning my recovery in very small stages, especially through goal-setting, I was able to control the fight and dictate the tempo of the fight with PTSD. In this way I was able to win the battle.

I had a very clear map in my head of the events on the day of the accident. I would say my recall was 80 per cent. I always felt that there was a reason I could not remember the missing 20 per cent. If you think of the brain as the most advanced computer you can imagine, it has an amazing protection system, a series of firewalls to protect your hard drive from dangerous viruses. Your brain is programmed to protect your system by not allowing you to process the most disturbing images of an accident all at once.

After the accident, I could not recall two important pieces of information. Those gaps in my memory were the most upsetting for me as I couldn't find answers to two questions that I desperately wanted answers for:

1. Why was I in the front of the helicopter on the return journey when I had also been in the front on the way to Waterford?

2. Did I see the clouds before we flew into them that day?

In the period after the accident, my physical injuries and my recovery from them were of most concern to me. Initially my mental injures were easy to park. I had to focus on getting out of hospital, on becoming as mobile as I possibly could. Those unanswered questions were more important to the legal teams than they were to me. They constantly brought them up but I was fighting for my physical wellbeing and refused to search for the answers.

The first bullet of information, the first clear recollection, ripped through my head six months after the accident. I was walking down the street in Galway when I passed the Front Door, Mark's old business, a place I had shared so many happy times with Mark and Damien. I smiled as the memories filled my mind.

Bang.

Suddenly, I was frozen to the spot. I couldn't move. I couldn't even talk. When I tried to speak to a passerby to confirm to myself that I was OK the words wouldn't come out. My thoughts had paralysed my body. My heart was racing. I was in an extreme panic. PTSD had entered my life for the first time.

In the space of a millisecond, all the events of the crash flashed through my mind. It was like something out of *The Matrix* movie, as if a jigsaw had been put together with the speed of light. Suddenly, it became clear. I had located one of the missing pieces. It was imprinted clearly on my mind, lit up in neon lights.

As I stood motionless in the street, I tried to focus on my immediate surroundings. It was lunchtime and the streets were packed. No one noticed that I had become paralysed by panic. Slowly, I forced myself to the opposite side of the street and leaned up against a wall.

I was half-expecting this visitor. And now that PTSD had finally arrived, I knew that somehow I had to get control of it.

I was processing this critical new piece of information. It wasn't Damien who had saved my life. Mark's good nature had played a huge part as well. I remembered how he had told me to stay in the front seat while he casually slipped in behind me.

My heart continued to race. I could barely breathe. It was a worrying sensation but I pulled myself together. I knew it would pass. Even having this insight while I felt paralysed by fear was a step forward. My brain told me that I was beginning to recover. It was now time to battle PTSD. It was time to deal with the mental scars left from the accident, in particular the survivor guilt. How come I had survived when my friends had not? Now was the time to put the jigsaw back together.

To begin that process, that journey, I needed all the facts about what had happened that day. I needed to make sure there was no disconnect between my brain and my body in relation to these events. This would afford me the chance to rid myself of mental scars. It would also allow me to process the elements of my recovery more clearly, to deal with certain new information and lock away other data I now had at my disposal. I wasn't aware of it at the time but taking that step strengthened my resolve and my mental ability to store away the pain that was still a constant in my life. Most importantly, my subconscious was telling me that it was finally time to fight the monkey that had been on my back for six months.

I had new information: that Mark had taken a critical, selfless decision. All things being equal, I should be dead, not Mark. I began to think about his decision. Many people said to me that my time wasn't up but I initially found this view very hard to accept. But as I began to think more about those events, I realised that they were right. There was no point obsessing about his decision. I could not allow guilt to define the rest of my life. I had to live it.

Boom.

Eighteen months after the crash, a second bullet ripped through my consciousness. By then I was well on the road to recovery. I was still ill but making significant physical progress. Mentally I was feeling pretty good. Then one evening I was lying on the couch watching TV. All of a sudden, it came at me.

Just as happened twelve months earlier I was playing the images of the accident in my head in high definition as they flashed through my mind like lightning. But this time I didn't have any of the feelings that had been associated with the last episode. No heart racing. No panic. I didn't feel frozen to the spot. But I had total recall of what had happened before we went down.

We had all seen the clouds that day as we approached the Slieve Aughty mountains. We were flying low on our approach and Damien made the decision to fly into those clouds. It all happened in seconds. Damien was aiming to fly out of the clouds just as he flew into them, which is exactly what he said he would do if he ever found himself in such a situation.

Why had it suddenly become clear at this point? What had triggered those images? I thought that I was on the home stretch of my recovery but the reality was that I couldn't fully recover until I had processed this information.

Mentally, I was now dealing with the most difficult aspect of the accident. If I had been able to recall it in the immediate aftermath of the crash, it could have totally consumed me. I might have been thinking, 'My friend made a big mistake. He caused this accident. He killed Mark. He has ruined my life. Why did this have to happen?' If I had been thinking like that at that time, my mind and my body would never have been able to recover in sync. And that disconnect could have caused severe PTSD, as well as seriously impairing my physical recovery.

Now that I could finally process this information properly, I reflected a lot on the decision Damien made that day. I thought about how we will all face life-and-death decisions during the course of our lives. My conclusion was that our decisions reflect our characters just as much as our reactions to the consequences of our decisions.

Damien made a decision that day which cost him and Mark their lives but he still fought with everything he had to try to save us. He didn't panic as he battled ferociously with the controls after the moment of impact. He reduced our speed after we clipped the trees. He kept a mental note of where we were. After we went down, he had the clarity of thought to ring the emergency services, alerting them to our location. If he had not reacted like this, I might not have survived.

The memory of Damien's valiant actions on the day, his refusal to give in until we had been airlifted to hospital, helped give me the strength to make a full recovery. This was my best friend. I was proud of him. This was how I chose to remember him.

No battle is easily won. You will take hits and the scars will often be visible. The lacerations will pierce you for days on end. The enemy appears under many guises and will hit you as hard as he possibly can. It's not about hitting back but about how hard you can be hit and keep getting up and moving forward.

During the first years after the accident I regularly had nightmares. I would wake in the middle of the night with my heart beating out of my chest, cold sweat coming out through my pores. I still get those nightmares from time to time but, thankfully, I never have any memory of what I was dreaming about. It disappears the instant I wake up. But I know I've been replaying the accident in my head. I will always relive those events but the big advantage I have in dealing with them is that I have accepted them. Otherwise my nightmares would have been much, much worse and my recovery compromised.

One key element of the crash stood to me. As we were going down, there was no panic. No screaming. I was genuinely not frightened. I didn't really have time to be. Even though we were in a seemingly perilous position, with death appearing imminent, dying did not dominate my thoughts in those crazy moments. It was as if life froze just before the crash, each moment played out in a freeze-frame sequence. That lack of painful and frightening memories of fear, terror, panic and helplessness – which dominate the mindset of many serious accident survivors – seriously diluted my symptoms of PTSD.

Any time I consulted psychologists or psychiatrists, one of the first questions they asked me was whether I had nightmares. I told them that I did and that they were about the accident. I was telling the truth. Yet I'm sure those doctors imagined them to be far worse than they really were. I was sure that an impartial judge would accept that truth. If not, I was at all times willing to take the stand and explain myself to a judge.

I had constant flashbacks immediately after the accident and I have them to this day. I suppose my life was so intertwined with Mark and Damien's that it is inevitable that there are many trigger points, especially when I walk around Galway. When I pass certain spots, I can see myself standing there with Mark and Damien, laughing alongside them, enjoying their company, luxuriating in our friendship.

Those images combine with flashbacks of the accident, particularly the wreckage. The wreckage and the destruction all around the helicopter are the most graphic trigger points of the day's devastation.

The best way to describe the hit from a flashback is that it concusses you. I have been concussed so many times in the last number of years that if I was playing sport, I would have been forced to retire.

I have profound sadness at the loss of my friends, combined with profound gratitude for my survival and the life I live today, and I have managed to keep that balance in my mind since the days after my accident. When I think of the two lads now, I can't help smiling. They were so full of life that it's hard to feel sad when I think about them. Yes, I want them here. Their lives were cut cruelly short but they lived life to the absolute maximum as long as they were alive. They packed more into those lives than some people could manage in three lifetimes.

So I told the truth when I said that I had flashbacks after the accident and that they were especially paralysing when I walked around Galway. But mainly it is my happy memories of the lads that stop me in my tracks. If anything, my flashbacks are happy flashbacks. During my legal case I was never asked to elaborate on that question.

Doctors often asked me if I sometimes talked to my dead friends. Yes, I talked to them throughout the whole legal process. I still talk to them to this day when I am mulling over any major business decision. This is not an unusual phenomenon. Anyone who has ever lost a parent or a loved one they were very close to, a mentor or someone who was inspirational in their lives, has experienced the desire to connect with that person. Let's be honest, most of us have mental conversations with someone else during tough times? It makes sense. You may be in a bad spot, hemmed in, you have a tough decision to make; of course your subconscious is going to 'consult' with someone who might help you to make a wiser decision about the question that's preoccupying you. I regularly talk to my dead friends.

I do not feel guilty to have survived the accident or even that it was me who survived and not one of the lads. The accident brought me through a transformative process and there is very little that I would change in my life today. If I had one wish, it would be that my two friends were still here on this earth with me. But now they aren't, I feel it is my duty to live my life to the absolute maximum. To do exactly what they would have done.

After the accident, the easiest assumption for everyone to make was that I was depressed. How could I not be depressed after losing my two best friends in such traumatic circumstances? But in reality, in the months after the accident, I had a profound sense of loss, which is not the same as depression. Such a massive part of my life was taken away from me in an instant and I missed it desperately. I still miss Mark and Damien terribly. I miss the conversations we had, the fun we had together.

On top of that great loss, I lost my independence. I couldn't drive and no longer had a driver's licence. I was dependent on other people, something that had never been the case before. My business had gone down the tubes. I did travel but when I was in Galway, I was effectively imprisoned inside my own house. Of course there were low times but I fought every single day against letting depression take hold of me. Being proactive was the best way to maintain my mental health. I never lost my sense of self-worth. I always felt there was a way out and better days ahead.

Yes, I was mentally scarred. I suffered from PTSD. I willingly answered yes to all those questions during the many medical examinations I underwent. I constructed my court case on this basis. My physical injuries were more complex and more open to debate but I was confident that no judge would rule against me on the basis that I did not suffer from PTSD. I'd like to think that I was honest, even if what I feel is perhaps a watered-down version of PTSD. Maybe I underestimate my PTSD in my own mind but I have certainly coped and come out the other side because of one key factor – I never let the accident take control of my mind.

I was like a sentry on a watchtower at a prison. No one was getting out and no gremlins were getting in. No demons were given a day pass on a low day. I chased them out again before they got bedded down. I had a really strong belief that if I collapsed mentally, the accident would have won. I had been given a glorious second chance and I would make damn sure I wasn't wasting it. The accident had taken a lot from me but it wasn't taking my mind. That was non-negotiable. Because if it took my mind, my life was over.

14

Healing

Sometimes people think that I'm squinting at them. Sizing them up. Measuring them with the focus of one eye. The reality is that I was born with strabismus, which is also known as squint and lazy eye. It is a condition whereby the two eyes are not properly aligned and can either be a disorder of the brain in coordinating the eyes, or of the power or direction of motion of one or more of the relevant muscles moving the eye.

Strabismus, which is present in about 4 per cent of children, is normally managed by specialists. My mother did everything possible for us but we didn't have the money or the backup for that kind of treatment when I was young. As a result, I taught my brain to switch off the vision in my left eye and look only out of my right. It is effectively mind over matter because I have two functioning eyes.

When I was lying in hospital after the accident, my eye condition often came to my mind. I felt that if I had the mental strength to be able to switch off the vision in one eye from a young age, I could now, by force of will, teach my body how to recover. I could coach myself to deal with my injuries, drill my mind to siphon the pain away and keep it locked away.

Sometimes when I write on a laptop for a certain length of time, I get paralysis down my right leg. I cannot feel my fingers. Does it bother me? It does if I focus on it. But just as with my eyes, I have coached my brain to ignore it. Rebuilding my health took many years. It has been sweat and tears, more than I could ever have imagined. Anyone in my position would have wanted to do the same but I was driven by an even stronger motivation – I knew that I had to make the recovery my friends would have wanted me to make. It was a long journey but I had the benefit of milestones and landmarks along the way. The destination that I have reached may have seemed an eternity away after the crash but taking little steps every day eventually got me there. It is like the philosophy of a young and successful hurling coach: 'How do you eat an elephant? By eating little elephant sandwiches.'

I never had any interest in sport or exercise, although some of my friends were sports fanatics. They played hurling, football, soccer, rugby, you name it. I hadn't a clue. Some of them were performing at a pretty high level but they may as well have been playing Scrabble as far as I was concerned. Going for a walk on the strand in Salthill was about as hectic as it got for me.

Lots of times I stayed in hotels when I was on the road as a pharmaceutical representative. After a while it dawned on me that most of these places had top-class gyms and swimming pools. I started to avail of those services. It was better than sitting in a room on my own watching TV. Going to the pool and sauna and jacuzzi afterwards was as good a place to meet people as a quiet hotel bar on a midweek evening.

After the accident, I had no other choice but to embrace exercise and fitness in an attempt to get stronger and make a full recovery. There were many stages in that process but for me the high point was in 2012 when I started to do Bikram yoga. Bikram yoga classes run for ninety minutes and consist of the same series of twenty-six postures and two breathing exercises. Ideally practised in a room heated to 105°F (40.6°C) with a humidity of 40 per cent, the unchanging sequence of postures is designed as an exercise to rejuvenate and strengthen the entire body, head to toe.

If someone had told me ten years ago that I would be a fervent follower of Bikram yoga, I'd have laughed at them – unless as a cover for looking at girls with nice figures bending their bodies into some tasty positions, especially with sweat dripping off them.

Now I am absolutely hooked on the practice. I love the challenge presented by the postures. It is a miracle that I am able to do it so well. Some of the postures are not easy but I love testing myself to the maximum and it gives me great satisfaction to compare my flexibility to people who are ten years younger than me. At times I go to different studios and my heart sings with the sense of fulfilment the class gives me. I sometimes want to shout at the top of my voice, to tell everyone around me what I've been through, that my back was broken, yet here I am now, contorting it into all sorts of different poses.

There were many steps on my road to physical recovery and an important aspect was my attitude towards medication. Of course you need a certain level of medication to get you back on track when you suffer such a serious accident but you have to remember the reality that is medication. It is great as a short-term crutch, nothing else.

In particular, pain medication and mental health medication can be very dangerous if you let it take control of you. I accepted that I required some medication but resisted becoming dependent on it to make my life better. I had seen this dependency when I worked selling similar medication. Would I accept it as part of my new life? No way.

When I left hospital I was prescribed a small army of pills, one of which was oxycodone. Having been a pharmaceutical rep for six years, I knew everything there was to know about that drug. It is an opioid (sometimes called a narcotic) pain reliever similar to morphine and primarily used to treat moderate to severe pain that is expected to last for an extended period of time.

On my first day out of hospital, my mother insisted that I take the pills although she realised I would question such a high intake. I swallowed what was prescribed for me and they knocked me for six. It was as if someone had hit me over the head with a sledgehammer. I was like a zombie for the rest of the day, not knowing whether I was coming or going. The next day, though, I knew exactly where I was going. And it wasn't down that route.

Of course, the whole thing is not as simple as refusing to take pills or painkillers on a given day. From my experience in the drugs industry, I knew that I needed to take a drug for at least two to three months straight to gain any benefit. I sometimes did that in the early stages of my recovery when the pain or my sleep needed a crutch. But I always tried to have a timetable or a schedule with a time limit mapped out in my head when I was taking something.

One thing set in stone was that I was never once on medication any time I was in court, as it would have clouded my judgement. By the time the court case was getting really serious, I hadn't taken any medication for a good length of time. By that stage, my body had become conditioned to dealing with the pain I continued to have.

Like an extreme athlete, I had found a place to lock away the pain, allowing me to manage it far better. It helped me to win the war but there were many battles along the way. There were many times when I was in great pain but I refused to contaminate my body with drugs and become dependent on them. As far as I was concerned, my body needed to heal naturally and taking those drugs – especially oxycodone – would not help this process.

I also needed my body to learn about its new reality. I had to become accustomed to pain and discomfort. What was the point in taking lots of painkillers since pain and discomfort were always going to be there? What was the point in risking becoming addicted to oxycodone? If I got hooked on painkillers, where might this lead? I had to learn to deal with pain and the sooner the better.

During the court case, I always had a plan. I wanted to keep travelling. I was hoping to go to Columbia University in New York City to do a masters. And being addicted to medication had no place in my plan.

15

Road

One day, I was sitting in a bar in New York when I got talking to a guy. The conversation didn't come from casually bumping into this fella. I had been eyeing him up for a while and had been trying to ignite the chat. When I lit the match, the conversation blazed.

I had been in the same place a few times before and I always noticed him in the same spot, observing everyone. He sat at the bar, drinking in the atmosphere as he sipped his beer. He never said a lot. He was sizing everyone else up.

That day, I went over to him and tiptoed my way into his little world. Before long, he had invited me into it. 'What is New York really like?' was one of the first questions I asked him.

'There are no New Yorkers in New York,' he replied. 'When would you see an average person in New York?'

He reckoned that everyone came to the place thinking they were special and that special things would happen for them. In his strong New York accent, he summed up what he felt really happened to those people. 'Most of them will burn out.'

I took to him straight away. I liked the way he looked at life and at people. He wasn't overly judgemental. He was perceptive and had a very clinical mind. His insight was sharp. He had his own dry wit. He used to call me 'Irish Mike'.

One day, I asked him if he was married. He pointed to the end of the bar and said, 'There is the love of my life.'

I was puzzled. I didn't understand what he was talking about. If it was the woman I was looking at – a cracking-looking lady – he surely wasn't married to her.

'Every man has a double life,' he said. 'Some guys love American football. Others love soccer. Others have part-time jobs or serious hobbies or they are obsessed with something. A woman will always be focused on kids and family and the home but a man is a different animal. That's why we lead double lives.'

He got me thinking and I thought he was right. If I wasn't living a double life, I would have suffered from depression. I needed to get out and do things, keep busy, explore. Feeling sorry for myself or having a victim mentality didn't interest me. I didn't want to be bothered by people staring at me in bars and asking me how I was. And then lowering their voice before asking, 'But how are you really?'

My mother and sisters were regularly asked that question about me but I wasn't going to hang around to let negativity suck the life out of me like a vampire. Although I still had the case to sort out I needed a distraction. I had the time and the money so off I went to see the world. It may seem crazy but I first took off the September after the accident. About three months after falling out of the sky, I went back up there again.

I knew I had to get away, it was that simple. So when my sister had a baby while she was living in Wales, I thought it was the perfect time to face down the fear of flying. My mother was going over to see Karen and I said I would go with her. She thought I was completely mad. She hardly wanted to go near an aeroplane herself after what happened to me and she couldn't understand my wanting to do it.

On our way back to Dublin, we flew into clouds and the plane started bouncing around in the turbulence. My mother turned to me, her face as white as a ghost, and asked me if I was OK. She was clearly terrified. I said I was fine. I wasn't going to go up in a helicopter again but this was different. If I wanted to get away and see the world, I had to conquer any fear I had of flying. So I did. Already I was moving on. The world was now my oyster and travelling would be my therapy.

Travelling was about more than seeing beautiful places and meeting great people. It gave me time to myself. It was the ultimate form of therapy but I did it all myself. I had the time to reflect and take stock but I got away from other people. I got away from being the victim but at the same time I had distractions. Travelling the world was interesting. I lived a double life while I was travelling, a secret life, so I cannot really argue with my New York friend.

I enjoyed being far away from home with no one talking about the accident. In Galway it was always a topic of conversation. When I was on the road, peace and quiet were my constant companions. No one knew about what had happened or anything about me. I often felt like a secret agent in that double life. Concealing my identity was a form of protection. I wanted people to get to know me from what they saw on the tin.

I was lucky because I had time and money to see the world but if I hadn't had those luxuries, I would have found something else to keep me distracted. I had to stop being the focus of my own problems, obsessing about them. When I was at home in Galway, because I wasn't able to drive. I was like a prisoner in my own home. There were times when I was in the house on my own for hours upon hours. Boredom was a form of torture for me and my antidote to boredom was travel. It wasn't as if I had the map of the world on my kitchen wall and ticked off all the places I wanted to see but it was a great help to have those trips to look forward to. The journey itself become more exciting every time I took off on a plane.

When I was on the road, I was able to be true to myself. I didn't have the worries or anxieties I had at home. Of course I had time to think but I was completely relaxed in my thinking and I found that the beauty and excitement in front of me washed away any negative thoughts. Beautiful places were like a sponge soaking up all the negativity and making my head and body feel far clearer and lighter.

I also found that you see the best of people when they are travelling because they are switched off from their normal concerns. We are all conditioned to live and act a certain way, but when people are travelling they turn off this conditioning.

When I was in New Zealand, I met a guy called John. He was drinking wine and I asked him if he liked wine.

'Wine saved my marriage,' he said.

I looked at him as if to say I didn't believe him.

'I'm serious, wine really saved my marriage.'

'I'm sure wine has wrecked a lot more marriages than saved them. How do you mean it saved your marriage?'

He told me the story of how he had been married for twenty years. His kids were reared and he was fed up of his wife. She couldn't stand him either. As far as they were concerned, the kids had gone their own way and they had no reason to stay together any longer. But they were stuck in a routine. They wanted to break up but they couldn't. The routine and the pattern of their lives were seemingly a better bet that the risk of the unknown.

They were both scared and miserable. He needed to do something to distract him so he took a wine-tasting course and he got really interested in it. Initially, he began bringing a bottle home so he and his wife could have it with their dinner. It wasn't done out of kindness or affection for his wife. It was just a gesture because she might have cooked the dinner.

As the weeks went by and bottles of wine kept landing on the dinner table, they began to have conversations about wines: the different tastes, noses, temperatures and growing conditions that made a bottle of wine what it was; the best wine-growing areas in the world.

Suddenly they were talking again. Laughing again. Being a proper couple again. One day, John asked his wife if she would like to come with him and his class to a wine-tasting festival. She did and they made a whole new bunch of friends. Before long, their lives were better than ever before They were happier than they'd ever been.

'So you see, wine did save my marriage,' he said.

It was a simple story but I was meeting new people every day who were telling me stories about their lives. These stories and the good times I spent with the people who shared them was like food for the soul. I felt nourished, energised, alive.

I met all sorts of people from every background, every walk of life. Everyone was different. On one trip, I met a cool American girl. I told her I was going to study organisational psychology and we really hit it off. She asked me if I would travel on with her but I had to head home a couple of days later.

A short while later, she emailed to say she would be in Rome in six days' time and wondered if I was interested in hooking up with her. I said yes.

Then she emailed back. 'Great, but I'm not sleeping with you.'

'Fine,' I replied. 'You're too young for me anyway.'

I booked flights and off I went. As soon as we met, we immediately clicked once again. We had an amazing connection and had mad chats about everything. She told me she was dumping her boyfriend. We even talked about marriage.

But when we were at dinner one evening she started freaking out. She had a cold sore. She had never had a cold sore before so she laid the blame at my door. We couldn't enjoy the meal because of the cold sore.

'What is my boyfriend going to think when I get back?' she asked. 'How else could I have got a cold sore? He will know straight away.' She stood up from the table and I could see the panic written all over her face. Then, all of a sudden, she fainted.

I had to jump up, scrape her off the floor and sit her on a chair outside the restaurant. She was freaked. I was frazzled. Over a goddamn cold sore. I'm not sure if it disappeared in time before she met up again with her boyfriend but I'm sure she took every remedy going to make sure it did.

I was lucky that I had the opportunity to travel. Its real value was the head space it gave me. Travelling allowed me the time to remove myself from an environment that only exacerbated my grief and feelings of loss. When I travelled I was with strangers. As far as they were concerned, I was a fit and able-bodied man. How else would they look on someone travelling the world on his own? As a result, I was forced to up my game. There was no comfort zone on the side of a hill or on a rocky trail. Physically, I had to adapt. Otherwise, I would be left behind or separated from the group I was travelling with. This was a huge challenge for me. It was fight or flight: a fight to regain my strength or flight back to my grief at home. I was fighting.

I was privileged to be able to see some of the most amazing places and structures in the world; the pyramids, the Great Wall of China, the Galapagos Islands. But it didn't matter if I was in one of those marvellous places, on a beach in southern Goa or in a dingy hostel in Rio. The most priceless gift of all was the opportunity I had to reflect. This time alone allowed me to make sense out of what had happened for myself. The answers weren't what the psychology textbooks laid down. Or what a doctor told me. I figured things out myself on my own terms in the way that best suited me. These are the sweetest answers of all.

Was it one lengthy, happy, luxurious holiday? Not by a long shot. I spent long periods in excruciating pain. The easiest thing would have been to go on untaxing day tours before retreating to a local spa or five-star hotel. To me, that was the soft option and would not have provided me with the answers I was looking for.

On one occasion I was in Patagonia in southern Chile,

clambering over glaciers and ice mountains. It was beautiful but I remember asking myself in the middle of the trek if I had gone totally mad because of the pain I was putting my body through. I pushed on because I wanted to prove to myself that I could do it. I was fighting pain during much of my travelling but I knew most of it was in my head. I was learning how not to let the pain beat me, all the time pushing myself away further away from the comfort zone the victim is always attracted to.

I did find what I was looking for, the key to my recovery, my own enlightenment. It had always been in front of me but I had never looked hard enough to see it. I found Michael Gibbons, found out who he actually was.

I discovered that the hardships and difficult periods in my life prior to the accident could all be channelled towards defeating the tsunami of pain, grief and PTSD that was trying to consume me. I was able to summon my survival personality.

I certainly hadn't found out who I was by the age of thirty but spending days travelling on buses and trains in faraway countries, sometimes not speaking a single word to anyone, was the best form of communication for me. I wasn't speaking to the people around me because I couldn't speak their language but I was talking to myself. I was asking myself the questions I could no longer avoid. I spent days upon days getting my head straight about what had happened and deciding how I would deal with it for the rest of my life and I found the answers and the strength that came with them.

At last, I felt I had found myself. The crash and the repercussions would always be there. There was always the risk of being struck down by grief and depression, the fallout of a horrendous accident. But I knew there could be no living in the past, that I would embrace the future. While I was on the road, this became the very essence of the person I had become.

16

Rebuilding

When I arrived in New York in September 2009 to begin my new life as a college student, I hit the ground running. I had an ace in my deck of cards and I wanted to play it at the blackjack table as quickly as possible. As far as I was concerned, all I had to do was open my mouth in the right place.

For some reason, an Irish accent is all the rage with certain women in the US. The best place to reveal your identity is obviously a bar, preferably an Irish bar. As soon as I found one downtown, I walked in and spotted two gorgeous girls, a brunette and a blonde. I am not a stalker but I planned my approach like a lion on the Serengeti, waiting for the ideal opportunity to pounce. As soon as a bar stool beside them became vacant, I moved in.

I couldn't just jump on them like a lion, even though I wanted to. I studied the terrain, mapped out in my head the best means of taking them down. I put on the strongest Irish brogue I could manage. I was plastering it on like paint.

Whatever you might think, the tactic worked like a killer move by a Russian chess champion.

The girls' ears pricked up. They were on to me like bees around a honey pot. I needed to stay calm. Focused. It was time to make another move. I picked up the phone and pretended to ring my mother, carrying on one side of a conversation with her in my Irish brogue.

Then it was time to play the joker. I had to let them know that I was funny. A bit of a chancer. A real Irish character.

'That lad is so lazy he wouldn't work off a battery. And as for that other lad beside him, if he had another brain cell he would pass for a plant.'

I felt it was going well. Now was the time let them know I was smart. Well, get them to *think* that I was smart, that I had a few more brain cells than a wind-up leprechaun. I started talking about maths equations. Tolstoy. *Hamlet*. Nuclear physics. Algebra. Agrarian economics in south-east Asia. I discussed Columbia University and Ivy League schools with the barman.

There was complete silence beside me. They were eaves-dropping on my every word, absorbing every syllable. I could feel their interest and their sense of intrigue. I needed to stay calm but now was the time to strike. I told the barman I had just been accepted in Columbia and that I was there to celebrate. I called for a tray of Jameson shots.

He knew exactly what I was at so he poured the shots and dropped them in front of the girls. When he asked them to help celebrate this Irish guy's entry to Columbia University, they could not contain themselves.

'Oh my God, are you really from Ireland?'

'Your accent is amazing. Say "Tree".'

They were taken down.

The blonde got up to go, said to me, 'Make sure you look after my friend now.'

I ordered another whiskey and pinched myself.

After a few minutes, I asked the barman where the bathroom was located and said to my brunette beauty, 'When I come back, let's get out of here and find the best craic in New York City.'

But when I returned, the girl was gone. Her drink was only half-empty. I looked at the barman and he just shook his head.

'You are a complete clown,' he said. 'Kermit the frog could do better than you.'

'What are you talking about?' I asked.

The second I went down the stairs, the girl left $50 on the counter, put on her jacket and left the place in such a hurry that sparks were coming off her high heels.

'Buddy, in this town, craic is drugs,' said the barman. 'Junkies take crack. She thought you were an addict, man. She probably thought you were going to rob her blind.'

I sank another few Jameson with the barman before heading home, alone, deflated and raging with myself. I'd absorbed lesson number one. No more talk about craic in this town.

When I studied in NUIG for my undergraduate degree in history, politics and sociology, I was an average student. That was more to do with my attitude to college at the time. My main interests were girls and partying. I ended up with a decent degree and I did better in my postgraduate course because it was more in my line of interest. I could have done far better if I hadn't been more interested in postponing responsibility for a few more years than in embracing it at that point in my life.

After the accident, I knew my life had changed. I had to evolve and gain new skills. I needed to find a new path, retrain and develop a new career. And the only way to do this properly was to go back to college. I remember making the decision while I was still in hospital.

The big difference was that I intended to go to college in the US. Initially I thought about Trinity College, Dublin, but I needed a fresh start and I felt that the US, especially New York, would be as good a place as any to make that start. If you looked at it rationally this ambition looked crazy: even the logistics of living in a city as huge and busy as New York in the physical condition I was in. What made it seem even more ridiculous was that I had an acute brain injury, caused by the impact of the accident on my skull.

If you have the courage you can always rebuild your life. This is what I was going to do in New York. At the stage at which I found myself, I wanted adventure and a sparkle in my life. Galway had become a bit tired for me by then. I needed to invent a new Michael Gibbons and Galway was not the place for this. I had found myself after the accident but not what I wanted to do with myself. The energy and buzz of New York were calling and I felt they would provide a fresh start.

When I looked at schools in New York, I fancied Columbia University, especially their organisational psychology programme. Three months after the accident, I went to stay with Stella in New York. Before I went, I made appointments with a few schools but Columbia was my preferred option. It was highly ambitious trying to get into an Ivy League school but I wanted to give it a go. If it worked out, great. If it didn't, I had lost nothing. The accident gave me the confidence to reach for the stars. Life was for living and I was going to live mine from that moment on.

Before I could even be considered for entry, I had to take an entrance exam and before I could even sit that exam, I had to retrain my brain and at the same time expand my knowledge. It was a massive test of will, mentally and physically, but it was something I had to do if I was to return to any semblance of normal life again.

Six months post-accident, I was still in a full body cast and my right arm was in a cast but every day, I got up and walked eight blocks to Kaplan University for a GMAT preparation course, spending three to four hours daily on one-on-one tuition. While I was making that trek I passed a homeless old man begging on the side of a street. The walk to Kaplan was excruciating and exhausting. After the grind of tuition with an injured brain, I would often almost be crawling on the pavement on the way home in the afternoon.

One day, I was barely moving when I passed the homeless guy.

He said to me: 'There you are again. I think I have problems but you're the guy with real problems, man. You're a space cadet.'

From then on for the next couple of months, that homeless guy had a comment every time I passed him. There were often times when I felt like going over and throttling him, especially when he added some extra venom to his sarcasm. It was tough to take but I had to keep going. I was still better off than him and to make my life even better, I had to endure this struggle.

With my brain injury, it was torture trying to study and upskill. My short-term memory had been seriously affected. I might ask the tutor about something one day and, a day or two later, I would have absolutely no recollection of it. I found it impossible to concentrate. I had to learn how to process data all over again. It was really frustrating and it caused me great anxiety. While I could see myself improving physically, dealing with a brain injury took a whole new level of determination.

I was already much better than I had been. I've forgotten a lot of this but my mother says that when I was in hospital after the accident I was very confused and it was obvious my brain had been affected. She could see it a mile off. I would think – and say – I was going to work or to the disco or out to meet the lads. For at least a year I would phone her maybe fifteen times in a row and ask her the same question every time. When people ask her about me now they really want to know how my head is. They think I can't be normal after getting those awful injuries. She admitted to me that this is what worried her at the very beginning. She was really frightened that the accident would take an awful mental toll on me. It was hard for her to watch me struggling with the brain injury because she could see what I couldn't. It was a very anxious time for her but I battled on and came out the other side. My mother tells people I'm normal now.

My New York tutor was really good with me. He was extremely patient but he needed to be because it was such a struggle. It's hard enough to get someone into an Ivy League school in the first place. Trying to get someone in with a brain injury would frustrate God.

To make matters worse, my right leg and right arm would go numb when I was sitting for any length of time. I have that problem to this day but it was far more uncomfortable back then when I was mentally and physically in worse shape.

There were times when it appeared as if I was wasting my time, that this was an impossible dream not worth chasing. I did the test a number of times and had very poor results. But I was determined that it wouldn't beat me and I tried everything to make it work. I started doing all sorts of puzzles, which helped me to concentrate. They also stimulated my short-term memory and forced me to develop a variety of learning skills all over again. Gradually, that proactive approach helped me to recover from the brain injury.

When I returned to Ireland, I continued to study hard online and elected to sit the test in Ireland but when I sat it again, I got a result short of the acceptable entrance grade for an MBA in Columbia Business School. It was another hammer blow but it didn't deter me. I knew I had to be patient but also realised I had to change my approach. The disadvantages that were holding me back needed to be turned into advantages. Sitting for so long doing the exams caused paralysis down my right side, something that really diminished my ability to perform well in them.

It got me thinking. For a start, I was sure that allowances were made for people in my situation. Secondly, I needed to step out from behind the test paper and the computer and make myself more visible to the people who made the big decisions at Columbia. They needed to see who I was, to understand my motivation in trying to rebuild my life and appreciate that I was trying to return to college so that I could make the most of this second chance I had been given.

I had a strong sense that these people were the gatekeepers to the rest of my life so I got on a plane and when I arrived in

New York I went straight to Columbia University and Columbia Business School. I guessed that the best time to meet the people in charge would be around 12.30 when they were going for lunch because they might have more time to talk.

I struck gold at both schools. I met the programme directors in the Department of Business and the Department of Organisational Psychology. They were my target audience and influencing their opinion of me was the key to unlocking the door and gaining entry to Columbia.

I don't want to come across as arrogant but they couldn't but be impressed. How often did they meet a potential student who was so keen to attend their school that he had travelled three thousand miles in a full-body cast to persuade them to admit him.

They gave me the opportunity I needed to present my case and showcase my determination and willpower. They were impressed and, a short while later, I was awarded a place on their organisational psychology programme. I now had a goal, a future, a new adventure that would take me away from Ireland. The thought of living in New York for two years was also a serious motivating factor for me.

However, not everything went entirely smoothly at this stage. Firstly, I couldn't realistically take my place on the course until after the court case was decided, which I knew was a few years away. Secondly, I broke up with Stella soon afterwards. We had tried out a long-term relationship but it didn't work. We had spent too much time apart with too many missed opportunities to build something together that would last.

We remain very close friends and I will never forget Stella's immense support during the most difficult time of my life. This is the girl who threatened to quit her job if she wasn't allowed time off to travel to Ireland to be by my bedside after the accident. For a week she slept on an armchair beside my bed in that hospital room. When I woke up in the middle of the night and tried to get dressed to go to a nightclub, or head off to work, or thought I was on a cruise ship, it was Stella who was there to set me straight. To this day we laugh when she reminds me of some of the incidents.

Then, when I went over to her in New York three months after the accident, she nursed me like a baby. She gave me my head space when I needed it during that time. She was a beacon of light when the darkness sometimes descended on me, illuminating a path out of the darkness with her soothing words and concrete guidance. When I was pursuing my college dream with the zeal of a crusader, she was the one holding the scabbard while I had my sword in the air.

I lost her but we never lost each other. Stella is one in a million and she will always be in my heart.

After the court case finally ended, I had enough financial security to follow my Columbia University dream. Two months later, I boarded a flight for New York in Shannon. I had a student visa and the US immigration officer asked me where I was going. When I told him Columbia University, he didn't hide his admiration. 'Oh my God, you must be so proud of yourself.' Then he shouted over to one of his colleagues. 'Hey, this guy is going to Columbia.'

'Well done, buddy,' the other guy said. 'That's some school to be going to. You must be some genius or something.'

On an earlier visit to the US I had overstayed my ninety-day visa by a couple of days, and the next time I went through immigration I was interrogated as if I was one of the head guys in al-Qaeda. How things change, I thought that day in Shannon. Now they're treating me like a celebrity. I was very proud of myself too If those guys knew half what I had gone through in the previous four years, they would have been singing that tune much more loudly.

I had every reason to be full of pride and buzzing with elation. The previous four years had been very demanding and draining.

True, I had travelled and seen a lot of the world but the court case was always waiting for me when I got back, on my shoulder, more like a gorilla than a monkey. Now it was behind me and my new life was stretching in front of me, with endless possibilities. It was a very positive moment. I felt great because I finally had my life back and felt fully in control of it again. I wasn't existing any longer. I was living.

When I landed in JFK on my way to start studying in Columbia University, I debated whether to get a bus or a taxi to Manhattan but decided it was a no-brainer. I was going to get myself a taxi. I deserved it. Plus, a taxi felt like the right way to arrive in Manhattan. As we approached, I got a lump in my throat – I still do any time I get near Manhattan. The skyline is so vast and the buildings so tall that they are almost hypnotic. You are instantly drawn to their towering magnetism, especially coming from a small place like Galway. Every time I arrived in New York I instantly became addicted to its energy. On that occasion I remember being overwhelmed by an intense feeling of excitement. I felt I was arriving home, even though I had flown three thousand miles from home. This place was going to be my base for the next couple of years and I had a really strong feeling that it was the one place on this earth where I really belonged.

I had arranged no accommodation, had no plan about where I might live, where I might hang out, how I would spend my time outside college. I didn't care. All that stuff would happen in its own good time. I checked into a hotel and began to look for an apartment. This is normally not an easy assignment in New York but to me it was child's play. After all I had been through, it was as easy as adding two and two. I had a place sorted within a week.

My new life officially began a couple of weeks later when I started college in Columbia. Life was great but studying in an Ivy League school is a massive challenge in itself. This was not like my time in university in Galway in the 1990s when I could cruise through my undergraduate programme and still end up with a decent degree. In Columbia, unless you studied like a demon, you were out the door.

The first semester was very tough going and the mental toll it exacted nearly killed me. It was a form of torture because my brain still wasn't fully functioning as it had been before the accident. It was a grim grind. My grades were very low that semester. I remember trying to write an essay one evening and I just couldn't get it off the ground. I had never done psychology before, whereas some of my classmates had excelled at the subject in their undergraduate programmes. They could write stuff in a couple of hours that it would take me days to get down on paper.

One night I went into meltdown. I was really worried that I had taken on too much, that I had jumped in too far at the deep end and was in danger of being submerged. I started to panic. I became convinced that I couldn't do what I was trying to do. I tried in vain to relax. I tried to get to sleep but sleep would not come. I was almost overcome by anxiety so I rang my mother. As usual, she was great. She nailed my concerns and anxieties on the head. She got me thinking straight again.

'You are the most determined person I know,' she said. 'Get up and do it.'

I spent hours and hours working on that essay. I put everything I possibly could into it and ended up getting a B. From that moment on, I knew I would be able to complete the course and it was up to me what kind of a grade I achieved.

For me, pain was one of the inevitable by-products of doing the course. Constant sitting while reading and especially writing and typing were tough going but I learned to cope and adapt. I improved my grades in the second semester and the improvement continued throughout the two and a half years of the course.

Along that journey, I met obstacles and barriers other than books I had to read and assignments I had to submit. Gradually overcoming the brain injury was an obvious first fence. Students in the US follow an APA (Academic Program Assessment) style of continuous assessment so doing computer work for hours on end had an effect on my sight. I had a scratched cornea from the accident which eventually required surgery when the problem deteriorated.

The Christmas after my first semester, a couple of friends from New Orleans came to visit. Some of the lads were staying with me; others were staying with college friends. One night we all went out to have a few beers. I wasn't drunk but I slipped on the pavement and came crashing down on my hip. I knew from the moment of impact that I had done some serious damage. I had always complained to the doctor about my hip. It was obviously brittle as a result of the accident but it is still very unusual for someone of thirty-four to break his hip in an innocuous fall. It's more the type of story you hear from an eighty-year-old person. But my body clearly wasn't that of a normal thirty-four-year-old. That was the reality I had to accept. When I was being ferried off to hospital in an ambulance, I had to swallow that reality like cod liver oil.

I have always had a high tolerance for pain but breaking my hip while I was attending college, while I was living in a high-rise apartment and while I had to negotiate my way around the busiest city in the world was another huge test. I was in hospital, all alone again. I feared I might have lost everything, not be able to finish college, that my future career could be up in smoke just as my former career was.

I rang my mother to tell her that I had broken my hip and she nearly died when she heard the news. She flew over to New York a few days later. I had warned her not to come but that's my mother for you. When she rang the bell of my apartment, it was all I could do to crawl over to answer the door. I must have been a horrendous sight for my poor mother. She said to me later that the pain in my face was the worst of all, that I looked like a man of ninety instead of thirty-four. She thought it was cruel. She and I went to the hospital by taxi the following day and there was terrible pain when they were pulling off the bandages. I admit I did think to myself, How much more pain will I have to go through? Will the future have more pain in store for me? My bones were obviously in a mess as a result of the accident.

When the surgeon examined me he came to the conclusion that I would need a hip replacement. I wouldn't entertain that idea. I know some young people, especially sports people, get hip replacements in their early thirties and nothing much is thought of it but I refused that option.

I had overcome more serious injury in the past and I knew that I could deal with this breakage without part of my body being ripped out of me and replaced by a piece of metal. I had enough metal in my body already. If I had any more I would be like the tin man in *The Wizard of Oz*.

I knew straight away what I needed to do, not physically, but mentally. I wanted to keep going to college, no matter how much of an impediment this injury was to me. I wanted to keep as much normality as I possibly could in my life. I had fought so hard and waited so long to achieve that normal life that there was no way I was going to let go of it now.

I spent eight months on crutches. It was difficult but it never really affected me as a student. I rejigged my classes. I did online courses. I pursued other areas of education. I went to Guatemala during the summer and took Spanish classes, for which I subsequently got credits. After eight months of partial isolation from my classmates, I rejoined them by the following September. It was as if I'd never been away. I put the coping mechanisms I had acquired to good use. I was up to speed in my course and ready for the next challenge, the next assignment. Bring it on.

I graduated from Columbia with a 3.6 GPA average. After the physical and mental battles I had to fight after the accident, I was interested in learning about how people deal with crises: what motivates them in these situations, how to manage people in the aftermath of these crises. I felt I already had an edge in this sphere and the sheer breadth of the classes in the programme allowed me to focus on areas of particular of interest to me.

I loved mediation. I studied crisis resolution and finished with fifteen credits from that course. The weekend classes that course involved were a real pleasure. There was a time when I wouldn't have looked at a book or gone near college over the weekend but this was something I looked forward to. The classes involved role playing and recording simulated crisis situations. Being constantly challenged by fellow students honed and improved my mediation techniques and an internship as a mediator with a business bureau provided me with invaluable experience. I was then nominated to go to work for a non-profit organisation in Miami.

From my accident I already had the raw experience of coping with crisis but after my master's in Columbia University and the hands-on development I had the tools and techniques to take it to the next level. I was able to use my own life history to help others deal with their life crises.

17

Truth

I don't know what it is about me. Maybe it is because I am bald and often wear shades that people think I look a bit dodgy. I have an intense stare but surely that in itself does not mean that I resemble an unscrupulous Russian drug baron. I'm certainly nowhere near as shady as people sometimes seem to think. The worst thing about this perception is that occasionally it goes deeper than my looks. People arrive at the conclusion after getting to know me. A good college friend of mine in New York was convinced that I was a drug dealer, purely on the basis that I had money and was a mature student in Columbia University. We used to joke about it but for all I knew, she may have thought that I was supplying cocaine to the entire campus.

It took me a while to open up to people with the truth and this process began on a trip to Las Vegas with a friend, Eric. We really cut loose and I would advise anyone who has not been to Vegas to go there. It was some blast. As well as drinking we spent our time chasing the loveliest girls in Vegas. We weren't there to slum it either. We found ourselves in Tao Beach, a famous poolside resort, located above the TAO Asian Bistro and Nightclub that attracts celebrities likes bees to honey: big names ranging from Jay Z and Heidi Klum to LeBron James and Jamie Foxx. The resort is so plush that you can reserve a luxury poolside cabana that features such amenities as air-conditioning, high definition plasma screen televisions with gaming consoles, Wifi and customised mini bars.

Or you can just lounge by the pool looking at the most beautiful girls imaginable. Not a bad second option.

Later that evening two beautiful girls, just as beautifully dressed, walked into the TAO bar. Quick as a flash, Eric was over to them introducing himself but they didn't want to have anything to do with him. But all I needed was a couple of seconds to play my trump card, my Irish accent. One of the girls, BB, who turned out to be a Puerto Rican ex-fashion model, was intrigued. Eric was charming her friend. We had got hold of two of the best lookers in Vegas. To make matters even better, BB was from Miami, the city where I was planning to live in after finishing college. Maybe I was jumping the gun, but I was thinking, 'Thank you God.'

We really hit it off and soon we were texting each other for up to four hours a day. We got to know everything about each other. Not long afterwards, she texted me to tell me how much she missed me and I started plotting our future together in my head. One night I texted her and told her that I could see us settling down together.

As soon as I did, the relationship cooled and the questions began. Basically she thought I was shady.

'Mike, since I've known you, you have been all over Europe and the US. You have also been to Brazil. All within the space of three months! You live in a nice place in New York and have just bought a condo in Miami. Who the hell lives like that – Howard Marks?'

Although I wasn't an international drug smuggler like Marks I could see her point. It was true that I was living life to the absolute maximum. It wasn't as if I was blowing all the money from the insurance payout. College in New York was an investment. Buying the condo in Miami was another practical investment. The weather was beautiful, the climate perfect for my back. I didn't have any major plan for my life. I was living it to the absolute maximum, intoxicated by survivor's delight.

'So tell me again, what do you really do?' BB asked.

'I'm a student, I'm telling you the truth.'

She clearly didn't believe me.

One a night out in Miami, BB told me a story. When she was growing up, a guy in her town imported cars. He was always flush with money and everyone assumed it was from his car-importing business. Then one morning, when BB was on her way to school, the FBI knocked down the door of the family home. The guy who was importing cars also happened to be importing cocaine in the boots of the cars. The guy also happened to be her father.

I guess something about me triggered a bad feeling in BB, so our relationship ended. We were both stubborn, too stubborn to try to work it out. I emailed her after I de-friended her on Facebook and got no reply? When I sent her a Happy New Year text a few months later, I didn't like her reply and it sparked an extended text fight.

I was crazy about BB but there were times when she absolutely wrecked my head. After I had spent £500 on tickets for a Broadway show, she emailed me at eleven the morning she was supposed to arrive to tell me that she was too busy at work to come to New York for the visit we had planned.

BB's dream was to start her own fashion label and she did have an excellent eye for fashion and design. The weekend she was supposed to visit, I had arranged, without telling her, for her to meet a fashion designer and potential co-investor. If things had worked out between them, I might even have invested in the business myself. I have a hugely talented backroom team to look after my investments and she would really have benefitted from their advice. In the end, I never even told her about that planned meeting.

She was a beautiful girl and we obviously crossed paths for a reason. Indirectly, she made me re-evaluate the perception other people had of me. I had never really cared about what others thought or said about me but being in a relationship with BB brought it up as an issue. I began to ask friends in New York if they thought I was shady. To my shock, they all said that they could not witness the lifestyle I had without having some suspicion about how I provided for that lifestyle. I laughed when one particular friend said she thought I was a drug dealer but I didn't laugh when I realised that other friends had similar ideas.

I clearly needed to put some thought into changing the impression people had of me. I had received a payout from the insurance company and consolidated it with a good return on some business investments. But the friends I had made in Columbia needed to know more about my past to trust me and acknowledge me for who I was and where I had come from. Otherwise, all my efforts to be accepted for the masters, the cost of the course, the expense of living in New York and the gruelling struggle to get a 3.6 average would be seriously compromised.

So I began giving more of myself. I told people about my past, about the crash and how going to Columbia was a critical step in rebuilding my life and self-worth after such a long-drawn-out court case. My American friends were always open with me about their past and who they really were and, even though I might be great fun to be around, I had given them nothing in return for this openness.

Although I had a strong urge to tell my story I had a stronger tendency to hide my past. My life in America cloaked my real identity instead of revealing it. BB showed me the downside of this secrecy. She was a girl from a similar background, someone with a matching sense of humour and free-spirited attitude to life. The whole experience with BB reaffirmed one of my strong beliefs: that you will find the right path in life by meeting the right people.

18

Ciara

Karen Brown

'After the accident, Mikey kept saying to me, "If I'm in a wheelchair, I don't want to live. I will never live like that." I believed him because it would mean his independence was gone. Then when I brought Ciara home, he cried and cried and cried. He was so guilty and remorseful about what he had said about the wheelchair. He said he would have swapped places with Ciara in a heartbeat.'

My sister Karen was twenty weeks pregnant with her second child when she found out the truth. Her first scan, in the Galway Clinic, had been perfect but the second scan revealed that an amnio-band, a thread-like vein in the womb, had come away and wrapped around the legs, cutting off the growth of the baby's lower limbs. The baby was going to be born with no limbs above the knee.

Karen always knew that Ciara was going to come early. In the end, as Karen says herself, she fell out of her. It was 5am on her birthday, 22 June 2008, when she went into labour. She delivered the baby herself, in her en-suite bathroom in Galway.

Karen knew during the night that the baby was coming. She could sense it. Her husband, Phil, rang my mother before calling an ambulance to come to the house. She had just returned from a few days in Spain with me when she received the call. She got dressed in a panic, and Karen sent Phil to pick her up (not a particularly bright idea as Karen was then at home on her own). After placing pillows on the floor and seeing Karen relaxed and in a comfortable position, she instructed Phil to keep sentry at the door to make sure the ambulance found the right house in their large residential area.

After about forty-five minutes the ambulance arrived in the estate and went flying past the house. Phil tore off after it like an Olympic sprinter. When he finally flagged the ambulance down, the personnel politely told him that for insurance reasons they couldn't take him back to the house where his wife was giving birth. All he could do was give them directions. By the time the ambulance and crew arrived at the house Karen had delivered the baby herself, very serenely.

Ciara Browne had come into our lives. She was tiny, weighing less than four pounds. Then she contracted blue jaundice immediately after being born, as the paramedics couldn't get to her on time so the umbilical cord wasn't clamped. That was a foretaste of the difficulties that lay before her.

Ciara seemed to spend an age in an incubator, when it fact it was only ten days in total in the premature baby unit (PBU). All the little creature had on her during that time was a tiny nappy, which seemed to leave her even more isolated and exposed. It was a very difficult time for Karen and Phil, although hey had a beautiful daughter, a little sister for their son, Oisín.

Staring and whispering had returned to the family but the focus was now on Ciara. Karen remembers that when Oisín was born she was inundated with cards and flowers, submerged under a tide of good wishes. When Ciara was born, there was hardly a ripple of congratulations. Karen barely got a card and flowers seemed to have gone out of fashion. It was as if her daughter's life couldn't be celebrated. It got so bad that people Karen knew well would cross the street to avoid her when they spotted her outside.

Karen remarks on the way people treated her so differently, almost like a freak. People the family knew well wouldn't even acknowledge this precious little baby. One day, when Ciara was nine months old, they were having something to eat in Tom Sheridan's bar. Karen used to dress Ciara in frilly dresses and tie the tights tied up at the back. She was sitting on her father's lap and there were two elderly ladies sitting across from them who kept nudging each other and turning to look. Even though Ciara was only a baby, she wriggled around, caught the dress, lifted it up over her head and dropped it again. Then she turned and cuddled into her father. She wanted to make her point. That is why Karen thinks she is so like me.

I would like to think I have a fair handle on the medical profession in Ireland, from my time as a medical rep. I got to see the industry first hand after the accident. I saw another side to it when I was mired in legal battles in my bid to secure compensation. I believe that, on the whole, the medical profession does its best. Successive governments have reneged on their responsibilities to the health service, leaving the sector high and dry. There always appear to be cutbacks in hospitals. No matter where you go, you hear stories of people being left to lie on trolleys.

Ciara's is a very rare case and surgeons and doctors in this country would have had very little experience in dealing with such cases. When a child has a serious illness or condition in Ireland it often happens that there is a big fundraising drive; then the child is sent, more than likely, to the US, to begin treatment. Ireland lacks expertise in many areas. To be brutally honest, the treatment Ciara received was sometimes so archaic that it was almost medieval. The doctors were doing their best but were hamstrung by the paucity of resources so their best was never going to be good enough for Ciara.

Karen and Phil were referred to a service provider in Ireland.

Because Ciara was still so young, only sixteen months old, her first set of prosthetics was purely cosmetic, to make her look 'normal' in today's society. As time went on she was provided with more practical limbs but the service providers were struggling to get limbs to attach to Ciara's body because of the complexity of the different lengths on her two sides so she always seemed to be in a prone position.

Everything they were working with was integrated with Velcro and pins. Karen and Phil spent two weeks in the centre with Ciara but because of the way they were trying to attach artificial legs, her spine was starting to twist, the early stages of scoliosis. They were shrugging their shoulders. She was becoming 'too complex'. Karen said she grew to hate that word, 'complex'.

Sometimes, life moves in mysterious ways. Or else you find a different way. A moment triggers an idea, even a dream. You have to chase that idea or dream. Even if it seems unreachable, you have to go for it. When you are desperate, don't second-guess yourself. Do it.

Karen was at her wits' end and they brought Ciara to the cinema one evening to relieve some of the stress. The film they saw was *Dolphin Tale*, inspired by the true story of Winter, a bottlenose dolphin that was rescued in December 2005 off the Florida coast and taken in by the Clearwater Marine Aquarium. Winter lost her tail after becoming entangled with a rope attached to a crab trap and was fitted with a prosthetic one.

The film got Karen thinking. 'Surely if they can do this for a dolphin,' she thought to herself, 'they can make my child walk?'

She remembers Ciara was sitting on her lap and from the very beginning of the film, she kept saying, 'It's the liner, it's the liner.' The dolphin had no tail and Karen could see what she was getting at.

That evening, Karen hit the internet. Hard. She began to research experts in the specialist area of acute prosthetics. Eventually, she found someone called Kevin Carroll, from a company called Hanger Clinic, based in Sarasota, on the Gulf coast of Florida. Even better, he was Irish.

Karen knew she had a chance and that was all she wanted. She said to us, 'This is the man who will make Ciara walk.' She found him on Facebook and sent him a message. She wrote that she was from the west of Ireland, that she had a three-and-a-half-year-old daughter with no lower limbs and was looking for advice. After ten days, she had heard nothing back. I told her to send him a picture of Ciara, a medical report, anything. She did.

On the Monday night, a man came on the phone with a real Tipperary accent. It was Kevin. He started to ask Karen questions about Ciara. He asked if she had an x-ray. When she said she had, he said to put it up to the light and take a picture. Before she sent it to him he said, 'I can make her walk.'

Karen replied, 'Are you really going to make our dreams come true?'

Then he asked, 'Can you be here on Thursday?' Karen said that she couldn't leave everything and get to Sarasota at such short notice. He asked, 'Can you be here in two weeks?' She said she could. Kevin said that another engineer would look after Ciara but that he would be there as well.

The whole family flew to Florida and I flew down from New York to meet them. They went to the clinic the next Monday morning, where they met Kevin Carroll and a prosthetist, Dan Strzempka.

Karen says, 'We were filled with confidence when we realised that Dan himself is a below-knee amputee as a result of a child-hood accident.

'There was no real surprise on people's faces that day, no shock like I'm used to seeing in Ireland. The population of the US is so massive that they see far more unusual cases than we see in Ireland or Europe.'

Because of having so many amputees, especially among soldiers, after the campaigns in Iraq and Afghanistan, experts have brought technology and medical science to a whole new level in the US. Some of their ideas are mind-blowing and their self-confidence is inspiring. Within ten minutes of Karen and her family arriving in Sarasota and meeting Kevin Carroll, he said to them, 'Yes, we can do this.'

Karen broke down in tears. She asked Kevin, 'Are you telling me you will have my child walking for Christmas?'

'I'll do better than that,' he said. 'I'll have her walking here this afternoon.'

That afternoon, after they had measured her, Ciara got up and started walking.

Karen Brown

'It was a huge turning point. We could see immediate progress for Ciara. They cast her straight away. They made sockets for her joints. They put her into her little "stubbies" – short plastic legs with no feet, just a round rubber pad, looking like a Guinness glass – and took away the feet she had. They put her down really small. At that stage, her left side was still in a prone position so her muscles were all seized. That got her walking. On Christmas Day that year, she pushed away the child's buggy that she had to hold her up and off she went.

'Before this, Ciara had prosthetic legs. They had feet on them and looked fine. She got the first set when she was sixteen months but they were cosmetic, there to make her look OK, somewhat normal. She was never going to walk on them. Now, she had legs that she was going to walk on.

'That was in December 2011. We went over again in May 2012, when they raised her by another three or four inches. She had new sockets. Originally, when they took her feet away – and there were no knee joints, they were fixed legs – they told Ciara that she would not be getting her bendy knees until she was at least six. She had got knee joints earlier on from her previous service provider but she couldn't work them.

'When they saw her again in Sarasota in May 2012, they were amazed by how well she was doing. She has PFFD, the medical term for having no ball and socket on the left side so the femur is higher up. When we went again in November 2012, they raised her again and she got the last set of legs. They gave her back her feet, which was a huge girlie thing. When we went back again in April 2013, they said that it looked like they were going to give her the knee joints nearly two years ahead of schedule.

'She is still adjusting. She often finds it difficult to keep up with other kids and can get quite upset but because they run off on her. But we noticed that her short side was growing. Whatever way she has developed her own hip, it has stopped the femur going up higher so the bone is actually growing, which is going to give her better leverage. There was originally nothing there for the prosthesis to connect to but now there is something more.

'Because she was able to get into a socket and walk more, this stimulated the growth plates. Ciara got so excited. She would say to me, "My bone is growing, my bone is growing. Maybe I will get my bendy legs." But I said to her, "Not until you are six."

'One evening, she was on the couch putting on her stubbies and she said to me, "Mammy, I'm going to get real legs like you." My mother was there and she said, "Ciara, you are special, you won't be getting real legs because that is how holy God made you." And she said, "Well I don't like him, Granny."

'I said, "Ciara, your legs are not going to grow. This is the way it is." Mike was over the following evening and she said to him, "Mike, my feet are made of rubber." I could see him thinking how he was going to handle this. I had already said to him, "Don't be soft with her, she needs to have the cold, hard facts, she can't think that her legs will ever grow."

'So he said to her, "But Ciara, my hair will never grow back." That was how he levelled with her and I could see her beginning to accept it.

'In many ways, she is a mini-version of Mike. She is the apple of his eye. They idolise each other. Mikey really pushes Ciara: "You're going to do it, you're going to do it." And she takes strength from that. It is almost as if she knows that Mikey has already done it.'

Ciara is an amazing child. I am not saying that just because she is my niece. She has such determination and confidence. When she was asked what was the first thing she would do with her new legs, she said: 'I want to walk. Then I want to run. And then I want to swim.' Kevin Carroll said to her: 'Well, you will be doing all of that before you go back to Ireland.'

And she did.

Ciara he has shown admirable resilience. She will have constant challenges to deal with throughout her life but she has already begun that process. Block by block. Step by step. No matter what, she will get there.

Ciara has accepted who she is. That is difficult for her as a child and will become even more difficult for her as she gets older and starts to develop her own personality and opinions. But I believe that she is already gaining a real sense of acceptance of her place in this life. You can see it in her demeanour. Despite being born without legs, she is the happiest child in the world. That in itself is a blessing.

The journey she has been on has also opened our eyes to what can be achieved when medical science is in tune with the human spirit. On one of our trips to Sarasota, we met a Brazilian teenager, who had been treated by the same team as Ciara some months earlier. He had been a perfectly functioning human being until he contracted meningitis at eighteen. To save his life, they had to amputate his arms and his legs.

Eventually, like us, he found Kevin Carroll. He underwent a similar procedure and has got his life back on track. He is now attending college in Florida. We met him and his beautiful girlfriend on a trip to Orlando that Hanger arranged. He is a total inspiration to us all but especially to Ciara. His story is a triumph of the human spirit.

Ciara has the family gene: immense willpower and a stubborn refusal to give up. My accident also helped us to be able to deal with Ciara. Survival is the name of our family game. I never tire of my own mantra about life repeating itself, time and time again, but as long as you are learning from these experiences, your survival personality will get stronger and stronger My accident taught me always to have my coping mechanisms firmly in place.

When I heard about Ciara, I was devastated but when I saw her for the very first time, it was like a lightning bolt ripped through my body. *Boom.* You hear fathers talking about feeling like this when they first see their newborn child. I am not a father but I experienced immense love that day.

So much of my life is now focused on Ciara. There were times when we all felt that life had dealt us a poor hand. But we have survived and got stronger and we have Ciara, who is one in ten million.

When she first came home, I did get very upset about what I had said after my accident. I was full of guilt and felt that I had let my sister and my beautiful little niece down. But I processed that and moved on. Ciara is one of very few children born in Ireland with her condition. It has had a serious impact on her life and that of her parents, her brother and her wider family. Yet she doesn't want our sympathy, or to be treated differently from any other child. Her attitude is more like: 'I want to do this. So get out of my way.' To see that strength of character in a child is inspiring and humbling.

Ciara has a motto on the wall in her home which reads: 'Some people want it to happen. Some people wish it would happen. Others *make* it happen.' This is absolutely true of Ciara and her determination. In the words of Dan Strzempka, anything is possible.

19

Surviving

I am sitting in the departures lounge in Dublin airport with a smile on my face, feeling a deep sense of satisfaction. Christmas has passed but the festive atmosphere lingers. The Christmas trees are still up, lights still glimmering in the branches, tinsel hanging from the ceiling. But my gaze is fixed on the runway, where planes are queuing up like ants planning an assault on a plate of food.

As the planes begin to take off, I wonder how many other people are watching them like I am. I scan the room and pick out some studious observers, their eyes intently focused as the steel belly lifts itself from the concrete floor and the plane points its nose towards the sky. What are these people really thinking? Are they wondering about the possibility of those planes crashing? Falling from the sky like a stone? I bet a few of these people are thinking along those lines. I observe one man very closely as his eyes track a 747 gradually disappearing into the clouds. He looks nervous, anxious. Like most people, he has probably pondered the terror of falling from the sky.

Everyone has an opinion about what it would be like to be in an air crash. It is a life-or-death situation, a catastrophe. The man I am observing closely looks like someone who is dreading going up in the sky. If so, his mind is surely full of assumptions and half-truths and images from Hollywood movies. He is probably visualising himself being sucked out of the belly of the plane faster than the speed of sound as the aircraft breaks up somewhere over the Atlantic. The reality is that most plane crashes occur at take-off or landing and the majority of people survive crashes. In fact the number of plane crashes has steadily declined in recent years.

A helicopter, on the other hand, is little more than a flying tractor. I would even say that any decent tractor shell would be stronger than the Robinson 44 we were in when we crashed. The volume of helicopter crashes is higher than everyone thinks, especially when compared with plane crashes. In March 2014, four people died after a civilian helicopter crashed in thick fog in the UK. One of them included businessman Edward Haughey, who was one of the richest men in Northern Ireland. He was chairman of Norbrook, the largest privately-owned pharmaceutical company in the world, and a former member of the Irish Seanad.

The helicopter came down in thick fog in a field in Gillingham, near Beccles, Norfolk. The crash site was only forty-five miles from the spot where four crew members died three months earlier when a US military helicopter crashed on a training mission in a nature reserve in Cley-next-the-Sea, also in Norfolk. The Sikorsky Pave Hawk from RAF Lakenheath was taking part in a low-flying training exercise when it came down.

Helicopter crashes sound like isolated incidents but they are occurring more often. In 2012, one database recorded a total of one hundred and thirty-three fatal accidents, involving the loss of four hundred and twenty lives. Military helicopters accounted for fifty such events and two hundred and forty-six lives, while civil helicopters were involved on eighty-three occasions, with one hundred and seventy-four lives lost.

Databases like this add to the ongoing debate about the safety of helicopters. In 2011, New Jersey Governor, Chris Christie, argued that it's safer to take a chopper than to speed around in a police escort, a practice that caused a near-fatal accident for his predecessor, Jon Corzine. Christie's comments sparked a debate about whether the car or the helicopter is a safer mode of transport. At the time data was inconclusive. Comparing the crash and fatality rates for automobiles and helicopters is an exceedingly complicated task, because the methods of data analysis for the two means of transport are totally different. The US National Transportation Safety Board measures automobile accidents per miles travelled, number of registered vehicles, number of licensed drivers and total population. Helicopter crash statistics, by contrast, are denominated in hours of flight time. One research study tracked down a number of experts to explore the topic but none of them thought there was a meaningful conversion factor between the two.

The study was still able to posit, on the basis of the available data from 2005-9, that, based on hours alone, helicopters were eighty-five times more dangerous than driving. When the study took a different angle and compared speeds, helicopter flying was deemed twenty-seven times more dangerous than driving.

There are numerous variables in helicopter crashes. As with our crash, fog was responsible for the four deaths in that crash in March 2014. Many fatal commercial helicopter crashes also occur during urgent flights and in risky weather. Fatalities in emergency medical transport crashes are higher than for other helicopters. According to some analyses of a ten-year period, working as crew on an emergency medical helicopter was the most dangerous job in America.

All those numbers may be surprising but the reality is that more people die in helicopter crashes than you would expect. Statistics released in 2013 showed that the global helicopter industry will be far short of its self-assigned, highly ambitious goal of cutting the number of accidents by 80 percent over the 2006-16 period, if current safety trends continue. Civil aviation authorities are striving to find new ways to improve this relatively worrying situation. Manufacturers are introducing new design processes and equipment as their part of the effort.

When the Air Accidents Investigation Branch (AAIB), which is responsible for investigating aircraft crashes in the UK, launched an investigation into the cause of the helicopter crash in Glasgow in November 2013, the preliminary report of its findings confirmed that the rotor blades were attached, but neither they nor the fenestron tail rotor were rotating at the time of impact. In its special bulletin on the accident in February 2014 the AAIB stated that the cause of the accident was that both engines had flamed out. Whatever the cause, ten people lost their lives that night.

It is another example of how lethal a helicopter can be.

As we went down that day, as Damien wrestled with the controls, trying to keep us alive, it would be easy for someone who had never experienced anything like it to imagine a scene of complete panic, chaos, mortal fear, total horror. But there was no fear or horror. Your brain goes into survival mode. Only in the movies will you see people shouting and screaming for dramatic effect.

As humans we have an inbuilt survivor instinct. It may not be at the forefront of our everyday life but it does exist and we all have it. Some of us have it more than others and I know I am one of those who have a very strong survivor instinct. The very fact that I am about to embark on a transatlantic plane journey, totally devoid of nerves or anxiety, is a clear indication of this. If anything, I am looking forward to it.

That is why I have a compelling urge to explain that any of us can overcome anything life throws at us. This is why I decided to write this book.

People have survived worse accidents than me. They have faced far more difficulties in their lives than I have had to face. But the most important thing for anyone who has suffered a traumatic experience is how you mentally adjust to the challenge, then how you embrace it. Taking the first step on that path is absolutely critical for anyone who is suffering, mentally or physically. Then you establish a routine and move forward.

I felt a giddy sense of excitement once I accepted the challenge to reclaim my life. I had had a life-changing experience and I was curious about how I would deal with the new life, the changed life that was the result. At the outset, it can be very hard to be positive but in this situation we can all rebuild a life as good, maybe even better, than the one we had before. Some people become liberated in their new life, realising how vacant and sterile their previous life really was.

It is essential to draw a line under the event to mark the spot where you can begin the journey back from a crisis or difficult time in your life. This is where healing truly begins. I think a lot of PTSD and survivor's guilt is a result of an inability to draw this line. I really believe that an ability to assimilate all the information around the tragic experience or crisis is essential if we want to minimise the chances of having nightmares, flashbacks, guilt and mental trauma. If we don't understand what has happened, we will keep reliving it over and over and over again. If we can align our conscious and subconscious minds we will convince our bodies that we have overcome the trauma and that we don't need to keep reliving it by means of nightmares and flashbacks.

I am lucky that I am a very positive person by nature. Some may even say that I am over-positive. My thoughts, conscious or subconscious, are always aligned and my body knows that I am healing. And that is why I have healed.

My flight is called. I drain the last drop of coffee from my cup, fold my newspaper and make sure my passport and boarding pass are to hand before getting up to join the queue. As I stand in line, I am smiling. Excited. I can't wait to get on that plane. To relax. To chill out. To visualise the new challenges that await me. I can't wait to go on living my precious life.

I take my seat by the window. I always ask for a window seat. There are plenty of people who have survived a helicopter crash who would see such a request as lunacy but I have no baggage or mental scars to prevent me from doing what I always did, sitting by the window. Why should I change? I have nothing to fear.

I believe my life has been enriched. I am endlessly thankful for what I have. I don't spend time wallowing in grief or mourning my dead friends. If I did, it would be a complete insult to Mark and Damien. If one of them had survived instead of me, I would have wanted him to live the fullest life he possibly could, to cram as much as humanly possible into that life.

I know that I too am only passing through this life but I now cherish every single day. I live it to the full.

My mother always knew I would recover from the accident and from losing Damien and Mark. She knew I was determined enough to achieve anything I set my mind on. She said to my sister the other day, 'As sure as I am standing here now, he will climb Mount Everest some day. I'm convinced he will.'

Maybe I will scale the world's highest peak. Or maybe not. I know I have already climbed my own Everest. I don't have to stand on the roof of the world to enjoy the beauty and admire the view. I do that every day of my life.

There will always be snowstorms and bad days along the way but life is not about waiting for the storm to pass; it is more about dancing in the rain while the storm is raging.

I am dancing.

And I hope you are too.